# *Where the Money Is*

## *A Fund Raiser's Guide to the Rich*

### *by Helen Bergan*

## BioGuide Press

Post Office Box 16072
Alexandria, Va. 22302

# Where the Money Is

by

Helen Bergan

BioGuide Press
P.O. Box 16072
Alexandria, VA 22302

Library of Congress Cataloging-in-Publication Data

Bergan, Helen
  Where the money is.

    Bibliography: p.
    Includes index.
    1. Fund raising--Research. 2. Millionaires--
Research. 3. Millionairesses--Research. 4. Biography--
Research. I. Title.
HG177.B48 1985      361.7      85-72141
ISBN 0-9615277-0-6 (pbk.)

Library of Congress Catalog Card Number: 85-72141

Printed in the United States of America
by Cushing-Malloy, Inc.

# Contents

# Preface

One day a development officer from a newly-formed museum in Washington, D.C., came to the public library seeking information on several names from the museum's potential donor list. When she saw the variety of published sources available, she was pleased—a little bit amazed. "Why doesn't someone put together a guide for fund raisers to help them find biographical information on the rich?" she said.

It sounded like a good idea.

Certainly, most fund raising manuals state very clearly that it is important for development officers to gather biographical information on persons with whom they will be in contact. These persons may be potential large donors, possible appointees to an organization's board, or leaders of a major fund-raising campaign. Whatever the reason for contact, biographical information is needed.

None of the fund-raising manuals, unfortunately, tell just how to gather this information. It is not always easy; at times it is almost impossible.

Some of the manuals say, in an off-hand manner, "Go to the public library" for biographical information, or "Consult a public librarian for help." Not bad advice, but it does not go far enough. It does not tell what information one can expect to find at a library, or what to do if the information is not there.

It is the purpose of this book to give fund raisers, development officers and others some concrete methods for finding the biographical information needed for an organization's or institution's fund-raising process.

In the several years that I have been Chief of the Biography Division of the District of Columbia Public Library in Washington, D.C., I have noticed that many fund raisers are taking the advice to visit the public library. There have been an increasing number of persons coming to the library seeking information on the rich. As funds from government grants decrease, researchers are looking for individuals who will give large donations. They want to know how a person or family acquired its wealth. What are the person's interests? Does the person have a history of giving to charitable causes? Is the person interested in music, or art, or health care, or children? What is the person's net worth? And, how can the person be contacted?

There is no ready-made directory of those who have money and are waiting to give some of it away. There are, however, methods to use to find the needed information. This book lists the most useful reference sources for this research, and gives other clues to information not found in books. I recommend reading this guide from cover to cover, marking the sources which seem the most useful. The next time biographical information on an individual is needed, the reader will know exactly where to begin the research.

I would like to acknowledge and thank Pat Feistritzer for editing this book. Gaal Shepherd of Chronicle Type and Design was the book designer. Clarence Mundy drew the cartoons. Many friends offered encouragement and ideas. I appreciated their help.

# 1
# Introduction

*The only question with wealth is what to do
with it. One important benefactor said very simply,
"It's a lot of fun—a lot of fun to make money.
It's not so much fun to have to manage it
intelligently. But the greatest fun of all is
giving it away." And that's the way I feel.*

*Avery Fisher*

Identifying where the money is and how to find information about those who have it has long been the work of fund raisers and development officers in a variety of not-for-profit organizations. It is the dream of all such persons to come across a donor with an attitude like that of Avery Fisher. He donated $10 million in 1973 for an endowment to cover the operation and maintenance of the orchestra hall now named in his honor in New York's Lincoln Center. Fisher, who made his money manufacturing top-of-the-line high fidelity equipment for the home, furthered his own interest in music and provided the city with funds for an orchestra hall through his endowment. It

9

was a happy blend, matching the donor with the project.

Finding the right donor for a project is not always easy. It used to be much simpler to locate available money. The government had a lot of it and was willing to give it away rather generously. But government giving is shrinking each year. For 30 years the government's funding to the arts and humanities, for example, grew steadily. It grew, that is, from the 1950s until 1981; the trend since then is definitely downward.

Funding for the arts and humanities increased from about $2.5 million in 1966 to over $154 million in 1980. Organizations were finally beginning to thrive when the trend changed. This change to a "new federalism" said, in effect, let others beside the federal government support the arts and humanities. Grant aid to many organizations was either lowered or eliminated completely. Beginning with the 1981 budget, there has been a drastic drop in all government support for not-for-profit organizations, a loss deeply felt.

It is conjectured that this decrease will continue. Each year a smaller proportion of the total national budget will be devoted to federal grants. The question for fund raisers thus becomes: Where do we go for funds to make up what we're not getting from the government?

There are only three basic kinds of grant givers: the government, corporations and individuals. Many corporations and individuals work through foundations bearing the corporate or family name to provide the much-desired tax exemption to charitable givers. The rest of the money is given directly by the individual. This is the largest portion.

Out of a total of over $60 billion given to philanthropic causes in 1982, the lion's share, almost $49 billion, was given directly by living individuals. Private citizens dropped this amount "into the countless return envelopes, outstretched palms, and collection plates that were passed before them that year. Another $5 billion was donated after death through individuals' bequests. Foundations, most of them also established by individuals, distributed about $3.2 billion more," as reported in *Forbes*, Fall, 1983. Compared to the generosity of individuals, corporations were rather stingy, with contributions of only $3.1 billion in 1982. Of all the charitable contributions, religious institutions received almost half of the total.

Personal philanthropy seems to be increasing steadily. In 1982 Americans gave 11.7 percent more than in 1981, and that year was an increase of 12.3 percent over 1980. Many small dollars came from the middle-class giver who supported the arts and humanities by attending concerts, by going to museums and by responding to mail solicitation. This all helped the needy organizations, but it did not replace the large sums lost from government funding.

To make things even worse, for the arts and humanities, for example, at the same time that government grants were decreasing, many of the attitudes of major foundations were changing. As social needs increased, much of the available grant money previously given to the arts and humanities went to causes which helped the needy. Waldemar A. Nielsen stated in the *New York Times,* October 26, 1980, that "organized philanthropy has become Calvinist, conscience-ridden, technocratic and bureaucratized. It has been painfully infected with social scientism. It has contracted a bad case of what could be called sociologist's foot." As foundation money, as well as government grants, became more difficult to obtain, fund raisers had to look around for other sources of funding. They looked to the individual.

Non-profit organizations of all types, including education and the arts and humanities, began to think in terms of the patrons who could, and just might, contribute large sums of money. They began to search for biographical information on those patrons to back up contacts for contributions.

Going to the individual for generous contributions was not a new idea. In the mid-19th century an example for philanthropy was set by Peter Cooper of New York, who made his fortune in real estate, a glue factory and locomotives. He gave his fortune in 1859 to establish Cooper Union in New York for free instruction in the arts and sciences.

There were also, of course, Andrew Carnegie's gifts of some $350 million given before his death to build libraries and to establish Carnegie Hall in New York. Then the stakes got even bigger. John D. Rockefeller gave away at least $531 million in his lifetime, and his example was nicely followed by his son John D. Rockefeller, Jr. He gave away about $474 million, to become a runner-up to his father in national generosity.

The list of giant contributors in the late 1800s and early 1900s could go on and on. How those early philanthropists decided where to donate their money is not fully documented. But it is clear that the typical fund raiser for an organization today must be aggressive in the search for large donations. How skillfully this is done can mean success or failure for an organization.

When the work of a fund raiser changed from skillful solicitation of government and foundation grants to skillful solicitation of the wealthy individual donor, the rules of the game also changed. Fund raisers found that locating the necessary biographical information on wealthy individuals was a lot harder than finding information on grant-giving government agencies or corporate and family foundations. Dozens of books exist documenting which groups and foundations give what kind of grants to whom. Library shelves are filled with literature about writing an irresistible proposal to warm the hearts of those who distribute funds for foundations. There is no comparable book to use in soliciting donations from the private sector. Nothing lists all philanthropic individuals, and there are as many ways to approach a possible donor as there are possible donors. But there are clues to discovering who has the money and, once that is known, other clues to information about that individual which might help in soliciting a large donation.

This book will furnish the clues. It also issues a warning. Finding biographical information on wealthy individuals is not only difficult, it is sometimes impossible, at least in published sources. The individual donor is probably the least documented source of funding, but do not be discouraged by this fact. In most cases, with this book as your guide, the information needed can be located through a skillful search.

# 2
# Who and Where Are the Wealthy?

*I was born into it and there was nothing
I could do about it. It was there,
like air or food or any other element. . . .
The only question with wealth is what to do with it.*

*John D. Rockefeller, Jr.*

*I*t should come as some comfort to fund raisers throughout the country that there is a lot of wealth in all states and the current inclination is to be generous with it. The term millionaire used to mean more than it does now, but now there are many more people who claim to be in that category.

A study by the U.S. Trust Company in New York, which deals in money management, estimated that there were 520,000 millionaires in the United States in 1980. That is about one in every 424 citizens. That figure was up dramatically from the government's estimate of only 180,000 as recently as 1972. Some estimates predict that the nation will soon have 1 million millionaires.

The rate of increase of millionaires in the population used to average 14 percent each year, but between 1981 and 1982 there was a phenomenal increase. In 1981 alone there was a 48.8 percent increase in the number of millionaires. Not only did the sheer number increase, but those in the much wealthier categories increased proportionally. In 1983 the IRS identified 9,600 individuals with assets over $5 million.

Fund raisers in Idaho, Maine and North Dakota will be pleased to know that there are more millionaires per 1,000 persons in those states than elsewhere in the country. Apparently, the less population in the state, the greater the chances of becoming a millionaire, especially if wealth is in land ownership.

Having large numbers of relatively wealthy persons living in an area is not all that matters. Often an area which has the highest per capita income may not be where the most money is given to philanthropic causes. A recent study by the Greater Washington Research Center revealed that although the Washington, D.C. area has the highest household income of any major metropolitan area in the country, it was only seventh in its charitable giving. It ranked last in a study which included Atlanta, Boston, Cleveland, Dallas/Fort Worth, Minneapolis/St. Paul and SanFrancisco/Oakland.

Minneapolis lead the seven areas in charitable deductions reported to the IRS, and Cleveland lead in gifts to the United Way. These may not have been major gifts, but they do indicate a community commitment which many think is lacking in the nation's capital city. Speculation is that many who live in or near Washington consider themselves "just passing through" with their loyalty elsewhere. They plan to be buried in Philadelphia, Pittsfield or Peoria, to quote the *Washington Post*. Even though fortunes may have been made in Washington, their bequests will probably be given to back home institutions.

Experienced grant seekers know they're more likely to get major charitable donations from very rich individuals. For all its high household income, Washington does not have many megamillionaires living in the area. Dallas, San Francisco and Minneapolis have more. Such super contributions from the very rich raise the averages for all.

Historically the greatest proportion of millionaires inherited their wealth. In recent years, however, that proportion has sharply declined. Many millionaires now make their own fortunes through a host of 20th century businesses that the Rockefellers, the Fricks and the Carnegies would never have dreamed possible. Although real estate and oil are good old-fashioned ways to make money, so now are computers, shipping companies, hamburgers, electronics, pizza parlors and ice cream cones. Possibilities are endless. Look at the salaries for football quarterbacks each fall. Old-line professions such as medicine and law now offer wonderful possibilities for huge wealth, and I've not even mentioned the numbers of rock stars who have pushed up the number of millionaires per capita. At age 26 Michael Jackson had an estimated personal fortune of about $70 million, and it is growing daily. And, don't discount the possibilities of extreme generosity by rock stars. Michael Jackson made $3 million during his 1984 Pepsico Victory tour. According to his manager, he donated all of it to the United Negro College Fund, the T.J. Martell Foundation for Leukemia and Cancer Research, and Camp Good Times, a camp for young cancer victims and their families.

To be rich is becoming almost ordinary; to be super rich takes a bit more doing. More than a few million is needed for the latter category.

In the first of what is to be an annual listing, *Forbes* came out in 1982 with their own list of the 400 richest Americans. It caused quite a stir. The issue was an instant best seller and it quickly became a collector's item. (Most of the collectors were probably fund raisers!) When *Forbes* decided to do it again in Fall of 1983, they stated that one had to have a "solid $125 million" even to get on the list. It took $150 million in 1984. Many names come and go from the list as fortunes rise and fall.

The 1983 *Forbes* richest 400 issue contained a reprint of a 1918 article in which B.C. Forbes, the founder of the magazine, had put together a listing of America's 30 richest families or individuals. (That was quite a task at that time, before the Securities and

# Where the Rich Live

## By State

| | Millionaires | Per 1,000 |
|---|---|---|
| 1. New York | 51,031 | 2.83 |
| 2. California | 33,681 | 1.49 |
| 3. Illinois | 31,138 | 2.74 |
| 4. Ohio | 27,607 | 2.58 |
| 5. Florida | 26,670 | 3.05 |
| 6. New Jersey | 26,565 | 3.61 |
| 7. Indiana | 24,345 | 4.56 |
| 8. Idaho | 23,797 | 26.65 |
| 9. Minnesota | 22,873 | 5.70 |
| 10. Texas | 21,051 | 1.60 |
| 11. Wisconsin | 19,006 | 4.05 |
| 12. Massachusetts | 18,015 | 3.10 |
| 13. Pennsylvania | 15,318 | 1.29 |
| 14. Michigan | 14,029 | 1.53 |
| 15. Tennessee | 11,705 | 2.70 |
| 16. Iowa | 11,602 | 3.95 |
| 17. Georgia | 10,886 | 2.15 |
| 18. Connecticut | 10,811 | 3.43 |
| 19. Nebraska | 10,462 | 6.58 |
| 20. North Carolina | 9,416 | 1.68 |
| 21. Maine | 8,337 | 7.72 |
| 22. Colorado | 6,868 | 2.53 |
| 23. Kansas | 6,822 | 2.88 |
| 24. Virginia | 6,769 | 1.29 |
| 25. Washington | 6,126 | 1.62 |
| 26. Louisiana | 5,981 | 1.49 |
| 27. Alabama | 5,501 | 1.46 |
| 28. South Carolina | 5,401 | 1.84 |
| 29. Missouri | 4,864 | 1.01 |
| 30. North Dakota | 4,598 | 6.90 |
| 31. Kentucky | 4,571 | 1.29 |
| 32. Mississippi | 4,557 | 1.89 |
| 33. Oklahoma | 4,050 | 1.40 |
| 34. Maryland, District of Columbia | 3,220 | 0.66 |
| 35. New Mexico | 2,825 | 2.28 |
| 36. Arizona | 2,756 | 1.16 |
| 37. Montana | 2,518 | 3.22 |
| 38. Oregon | 2,376 | 0.97 |
| 39. Hawaii | 2,077 | 2.26 |
| 40. Delaware | 1,946 | 3.29 |
| 41. Rhode Island | 1,449 | 1.54 |
| 42. Vermont | 1,105 | 2.23 |
| 43. West Virginia | 1,046 | 0.55 |
| 44. Alaska | 784 | 1.76 |
| 45. Arkansas | 748 | 0.34 |
| 46. South Dakota | 701 | 0.99 |
| 47. Utah | 665 | 0.51 |
| 48. New Hampshire | 603 | 0.70 |
| 49. Nevada | 223 | 0.34 |
| 50. Wyoming | 84 | 0.19 |

Exchange Commission made disclosure a necessity for public companies.) These *Forbes* annual issues make fascinating reading, even for non-fund raisers. Those who didn't move fast enough to get their own copies might want to spend an afternoon reading them at the public library.

In addition to the *Forbes* articles, a more specialized listing was published by *Town and Country* magazine in September, 1979. The original intent was to include all wealthy Texans, but there were so many that only those with over $30 million ended up on the list.

The highest paid executives of 1983 were listed in *Business Week* in its annual pay survey published in the May 7, 1984 issue. The highest paid executive made $13 + million in salary and other benefits that year. The year before, the top salary was a lot higher—$51.2 million! These salaries may not be typical, but they do indicate some rather dramatic possibilities for philanthropy. Finding which of these well-paid executives may be interested in a particular cause may be worth investigating. Those who wish to practice biographical research skills might use these names as starters. Probably every fund raiser in the country is doing the same thing!

*Forbes* magazine also does a listing of 800 firms and the compensation paid their chief executive officers. The issue in June each year gives company name, name of chief executive officer, age, rank, compensation breakdown by salary and other benefits, years with company, years as chief executive officer, place of birth and business background.

Having the wealth and being willing to give some of it away are not always synonymous. It is often quite easy to identify the persons in your community who have the most money, but it is not nearly as easy to determine those persons' giving patterns. The fund raiser's task is to find biographical clues about the individual which will help to connect the person or family with the organization needing a large donation. If a donor wants to give a few thousand dollars to your cause, it does not matter very much how the money was made or how the donor is viewed by the community. The money is absorbed into the total budget and

17

is not identified with a particular donor. It matters a lot more, however, if that donor wants to give several million dollars to fund a new wing of a hospital with the stipulation that the area be given his name. At this point, the source of money and the community's impression of the donor make a difference. The fund raiser, although understandably delighted with the potential gift, must do a quiet investigation before an agreement can be made about the proposed gift and the name for the new facility.

Sometimes it is more than just the name of a building which is in question; it may be the name of the whole institution. In the early 1970s Jack M. Eckerd gave $10 million to Florida Presbyterian College in St. Petersburg, Florida. It is now Eckerd College.

Sometimes also, a major donor will give a large contribution to an institution to "pay off an old debt." Such was the case when James Michener, the author of many best-sellers, gave Swarthmore College $2 million recently. He said he gave it because he had entered that college almost 60 years ago on a $2,000 scholarship. "That's one thousand to one," he said to explain the arithmetic of his gift. "Just about the financial value of a good liberal arts education."

Keep reading for information on how to put together a biographical profile on potential major donors.

# 3
# Why Biographical Information Is Necessary

*I made the money.*
*You guys will have to figure out*
*how to spend it.*

*John Donald MacArthur*

Seeking biographical information is a never-ending job for a development staff. Although you may think this information is needed only about those being courted for a large contribution, it is just as necessary to be informed about persons who may be appointed to an organization's board or asked to chair a major fund-raising campaign. The importance of these choices cannot be underestimated. How those persons are perceived by the community will be a major determining factor in the success or failure of a fund-raising campaign.

Regardless of the reason for gathering the names of wealthy, or at least influential persons, the need for background information is the same. It is very necessary.

As far back as 1933 this point was made by John D. Rockefeller, Jr. in a speech given before the Citizen's Family Welfare Committee of New York. He said:

> It is a great help to know something about the person whom you are approaching. You cannot deal successfully with all people the same way. Therefore, it is desirable to find out something about the person you are going to—what his interests are, whether you have any friends in common, whether he gave last year, if so, how much he gave, what he might be able to give this year, etc. Information such as this puts you more closely in touch with him and makes the approach easier.

If Rockefeller expected those who approached him to do their homework first, the same is just as true of those who have less money to give and who are less known. The approached person will be flattered by your knowledge of him or her.

Let's separate for a bit the information needed on a major donor and that needed for a person serving on an organization's board or campaign program. A major donor may be an old grouch, just as long as he cheerfully writes out an occasional large check. Such a person may be less desirable as a member of the board of trustees (unless, of course, that is the *only* way the checks would keep coming). The person would be a liability as the director of a fund-raising campaign which requires an out-going personality capable of bringing in many wealthy donors. The information you are seeking on a person will, in some cases, depend on why you want it. It will be different for donors than for those in leadership roles.

Before seeking a person for any role in your organization, let's say for chair of the annual fund-raising drive, the development staff should sit down and determine qualities which will be most needed. Much has been written about the traits needed for persons in various roles. While gathering information, both in person and from published sources, watch for characteristics such as those detailed below.

Using a very pragmatic approach, Irving Warner, author of *The Art of Fundraising* and a 35-year practitioner of that profession, puts being rich on top of a list of qualities needed for board members and campaign chairs. He writes that being rich and having clout almost always go together, making this person an ideal choice. That point could be argued, I suppose, but it is likely that the rich person will have social contacts, may be politically connected, and probably will know other community leaders—all pluses in influencing potential major donors.

Other important qualities, according to Warner, are being well-liked, being a true believer in the cause, being well-organized, being a good speaker, and being "fearless."

Another fund-raiser professional and author, Jerold Panas, in *Mega Gifts, Who Gives Them, Who Gets Them,* states that major donors give their largest gifts to those institutions where they serve on boards or in some official capacity. He says that not all on a board will be able to make what he calls a "sacrificial gift," but most of those large gifts come from those deeply involved in an organization.

Panas's qualities for a board member are three W's: Work, Wisdom and Wealth. He states that finding a person with those qualities is becoming more difficult. He recommends that poten-

tial board members who show these qualities, plus promise and resolve, be pursued and romanced with all the ardor used in pursuing a large donor, for often they become just that.

Panas states that 20 out of 30 persons who gave $1 million gifts in 1983 were on the board of directors of the recipient institution. It is possible, of course, to invite persons to *become* interested in your institution. In 1982 Beloit College in Wisconsin used this approach. They ran ads in the *Wall Street Journal* and the *New York Times* asking for a benefactor willing to invest one million dollars in the college, following an example set by D.K. Pearsons at the turn of the century. They received at least five potential benefactors and the college president was up front in talking about a "long-range proposition."

Finding the "perfect" person for the organization's positions is not just a matter of pulling a name from a hat, even though advertising might help. He or she should be presented with a logical reason for affiliation with the organization. While gathering information on prospective persons, always look for the "hook" which will connect the individual with the group. Try to determine if the person being researched is really as good as the reputation. What are the main virtues of the person? How do they relate to your needs? The better your research, the easier it will be to answer the necessary questions regarding your organization's leadership.

After researching several possibilities, it is time for a meeting of the staff, or a selection committee, to evaluate the data. Decide which person will be approached first, then list the others in descending order, in case your first choice declines.

Call the chosen person for an interview, but don't spring the honor (or the task) about to be bestowed over the phone. This needs the personal touch. Because persons of wealth or outstanding capability are very busy people, it may be difficult to set up an appointment. Use the best person in your organization to make the contact for the interview. This may be the person (or friend) who suggested the name in the first place. Although the request for an actual gift may best come from the chief executive officer, a personal contact with a friend may open the door initially.

If your first candidate for a position declines, it is a good idea to involve that person further by asking recommendations for someone else to serve in a needed capacity. Let the person know that you still need his or her support. Perhaps your first choice would be available to speak at a kick-off banquet, to solicit other acquaintances or, at least, to consider giving a sizable donation. The person may be asked about the possibility of service at a later time.

Qualities you are looking for in your fund-raising efforts will be similar to those needed when seeking a top executive of any business. Irving Warner lists qualities you will want to watch for. They include professional standing in the organization's field; personal prestige, credibility and visibility; professional skills needed by the organization (law, accounting, investment and building skills); ability and willingness to contribute big dollars; ability and willingness to solicit others to do the same; political influence, wisdom, intelligence and leadership. Keep these qualities in mind while doing research on a person. Watch for evidence of these traits. You may wish, while doing research, to develop a chart to use in evaluating a person's potential.

Warner emphasizes the desirability of finding a person with most of those skills, but he somewhat contradicts himself by saying that wealth is still the most needed asset.

He emphasizes choosing persons who are important in the field in which the organization operates, but sees this as a secondary qualification to wealth. This may sound crass, but he reasons that wealth attracts wealth and that is, after all, what fund raising is all about. He says that any organization should seek out rich persons, then try to find a reason for their interest in the cause.

This reason for interest, or "hook" to your organization, should be a person's intense concern for your cause. Panas states that the chief motivation factor in giving large gifts to an organization is a strong belief in the mission of that institution. According to Panas, who interviewed several large donors, there was not a close second reason. The donor had to have a high regard for the staff leadership and a feeling that the institution was fiscally stable, but a belief in the organization's objectives is what caused a donor to exercise his community responsibility and civic pride by donating time or money to further that cause. The person's actual involvement in the work of the organization, perhaps through its fund-raising program or board membership, can be very beneficial also.

If further evidence is needed to convince a fund raiser that gathering information on a prospective donor or board member is necessary (even after John D. Rockefeller, Jr. said it was!), here it is. It has been determined that one-third of the funds raised in a campaign program will come from the top 10 to 15 gifts. The second one-third will come from the next 100 to 125 gifts. The last one-third will come from *all* other gifts.

Time spent in researching and courting the top third will pay off. That group must be convinced that they can share in the dream which your organization or campaign presents. They must be led to believe in the objectives of your institution and in its ability to make some significant contribution to the furthering of those objectives or that dream.

Those identified as being in the potential top third should become the target of special attention or "cultivation." Such persons should be courted with great attention, but finding relevant information about them must come first.

# 4

# How to Add Names
# to Your Prospect List

*Money attracts money.*

*Yiddish Proverb*

Let us assume that most organizations which have been going for some time already have a list of donors or potential donors. Knowing the names of those persons is half the battle. Although the main point of this publication is to tell you how to find information on a person *after* you have the name, it is also useful to include some ideas for name gathering. How does an organization, or an institution, expand its potential prospect list?

Perhaps the best source for new names is contact with those already affiliated with your organization. Those wealthy persons on your board, or involved in some other way, may be solicited for names of other potential large donors among their acquaintances. There is often, it seems, a sense of fraternity among the rich. Many know each other and may have become acquainted

25

while working on other charitable causes. Ask your current friends to write down all potential acquaintances who may also become involved with your organization, no matter how obscure the connection. Use the "brainstorming" technique to come up with additional names.

This personal contact approach works best because it is harder to say no to a friend than to a stranger. A friend can offer the prospect any number of reasons for involvement beyond the possible tax deduction: a spot on an organization's board, a chance for public recognition for a contribution, or even the joy of having one's name forever on a stone! Such an offer, accepted by enough people in 1981 to raise $500,000 for Washington's National Cathedral, enabled donors to purchase a stone in the massive structure. $250 got them a small stone; $1,250 a much larger one. Of course, they have to consult a directory to find "their" stone, but it will be there FOREVER!

One wealthy friend may suggest to another that he or she endow an orchestra chair of a symphony orchestra. That will cost $250,000 at Washington's National Symphony Orchestra. "If you buy a chair," said the symphony's executive director Henry Fogel, "your name will go on in perpetuity. One hundred years from now your name will still be on that chair." How better to buy a bit of immortality?

An invitation, by a friend, to become a member of the board of that symphony may require a commitment to give or raise $10,000 annually. What one friend can tell another is that it is a nice feeling to be a member of that exclusive group. And, there are perks. There can be opening night receptions, the best seats in the house, and the chance to meet performers and artists. Some organizations offer free attendance, free parking (no small thing in some cities) and an "insider" feeling which comes with involvement and contribution.

Those already involved in your organization can tell their friends about the chances for public recognition offered by your group. These can be numerous. The program from a recent performance of Shakespeare's "Henry V" listed some of those possibilities offered by the Washington Folger Theatre. Those corporations, foundations and individuals who offered "major assistance" are listed first. This is followed by a listing of the 10/20 Club, a group of supporters who have made a substantial gift to the Folger Shakespeare Library to help underwrite the expenses of the Folger Theatre. Under a category called Folger Theatre Guild Members, backers, patrons, benefactors, sponsors and donors are noted. There is even a listing of a new committee, the Lawyers' Committee, apparently just for wealthy, theatre-loving attorneys. (Does the Lawyers' Commmittee know that in the Folger's gift shop they are selling a T-shirt with a quote from "Henry V?" It states, "The first thing to do, let's kill all the lawyers." In Washington, where the ratio of lawyers to the common man is the highest in the country, the T-shirt is a best seller.)

In addition to having one's name on an organization's printed matter, there is the even more exciting chance to have one's name on a structure. Some people like this idea, some apparently don't. The question of public recognition of one's generosity or the wish to stay anonymous is often a delicate balance.

Alice Tully of New York City, who inherited her money from the Corning glass fortunes, gave $4,500,000 for construction of a recital hall primarily for chamber music in Lincoln Center. She had planned that it would be an anonymous gift, but John D. Rockefeller III persuaded her to allow the hall to be named in her honor. Now the name of Alice Tully is known throughout the country for this generous contribution. Miss Tully had since the late 1940s been a generous contributor to many philanthropic activities, but the idea of the chamber music hall really caught her attention. After Rockefeller convinced her to use her name on the hall, she took a look at the plans for the auditorium and decided the colors of the seats were not to her liking. She felt they were not cozy enough. She convinced the designers to make a change to a softer color, and now everyone is apparently content. It was a small change to keep a $4.5 million donor happy.

In the early 1980s the National Gallery in Washington hired development officers to research the giving abilities of all probable $1 million donors in the entire country. This included a group of 70 supporters already known to the Gallery as the "Collectors

Committee," whose individual members contribute $5,000 per year for the purchase of art. Using as many sources as could be found, other potential large donors were identified and researched. (More about some of those research techniques later.)

Aside from this personal contact with those already considered friends, there are other ways to locate wealthy donors right in your own back yard by using readily available published sources.

One fairly easy way to identify local wealthy persons is through real estate directories which list the value of property and tell who lives there. It's a fairly accurate assumption that one who lives in a million dollar house has other assets available. Start your search in your local public library. If that is very small, you may have to be referred to a larger library in a county seat or regional location.

In many communities there are city assessment directories which give property values along with the owner's name and mailing address.

Finding out information on a person's wealth through access to real estate directories may sound sneaky, like an invasion of privacy, but these records are public documents and it is easy to gain access to them. They are published for any number of reasons. Your use of them to find wealthy donors is an appropriate use for the materials. If the public library does not have copies of these city assessment books, ask there where you may find them.

Keep in mind, though, that there are surprises in those real estate records. Use them, but be a bit cautious. Some very valuable properties have been inherited by the persons currently living in them. The current residents may not have much wealth beyond the value of their property. Also, the person living on choice property may not fit your standards for a potential donor. One recent example of this occurred in suburban Washington, D.C., where a very expensive house was owned by the professional burglar who had burgled his way to economic fortune. Only after he shot and killed a prominent physician, and was himself caught, did his neighbors find out his real background. That kind of detail will not be shown in the real estate assessment records. Be prepared to do further research on any names you take from that source. Don't assume too much from the cold facts found there. There are also *Haines Criss-Cross Directories* for 50 major cities in the United States. These include listings of residences and businesses by street and house numbers as well as by telephone sequence. Only persons with listed telephone numbers will be included, so many persons on your donor list may not appear here. Nevertheless,used with other directories, the *Haines Directories* serve a useful purpose in your research.

City directories in more than 1,400 areas in this country are published by R.L. Polk & Company. Information given for each address are the names of the persons who live there, whether the resident owns or rents the property, and the occupations and employers of the residents. These directories come out very irregularly. Because of the nature of our transient society, make sure that the city directory you use is fairly current.

Another way to identify where the money is in your community is to use professional directories. There may be local directories in many professions as well as national directories with geographical indexes which you can use to find local persons.

Two examples of these professional directories with geographic listings are the *American Medical Directory* and the *Martindale-Hubbell Law Directory*. To check which other professional associations have membership directories with biographical information, consult the *Encyclopedia of Associations*. This contains a host of information on almost every subject. Once you begin to use it, you will find it answers, or at least leads you to someone who can answer, many of your questions. These professional associations may be your best source to find persons who have a particular professional affinity to the work of your organization.

Don't overlook the yellow pages of your local telephone directory which list members of professions together. This makes no judgment about the wealth of those listed, of course, but it may serve as a beginning for your name-gathering process. Match up your organization's area of interest with those professions which should be concerned about what you are doing.

To find socially prominent, often wealthy, persons in your area, consult the *Social Register* published in New York for 13 large cities, even though not much information is given for each entry. The register's main purpose seems to be locating other persons also listed. It includes the name, spouse's name with maiden name, clubs, children and their schools, current address (with off-season addresses also given), and phone number (even those not listed in local telephone directories). The index to maiden names in the *Social Register* can be extremely useful. It might quickly identify where the family fortune originated.

Sometimes it is possible to get the membership directories for organizations such as the Junior League and other local clubs often identified with wealthy city residents. If a member of your board, or someone already involved with your organization, is a member of one of those clubs, he or she may be willing to share the membership list or directory with your development office.

It will come as no surprise that if a person can be identified as giving to one charitable cause, he or she may give to another. Check the donor or patron lists on symphony and theatre programs. Take a good look at letterheads mailed out from other non-profit groups in your area. Many list their prominent sponsors. Call these groups and ask for a list of their board of directors. Such information is easy to obtain.

Some organizations, such as museums and symphonies, publish an annual report listing major donors. In some areas, for example, the Jewish United Fund makes available a list of donors which includes the amount of their contribution to that organization.

Local newspapers and periodicals are an excellent and continuing source for adding new names of wealthy donors to your list. The social pages, or whatever they are now called in your area, tell who gives the fancy parties, who goes to them, and who hosts the local fund-raising charitable functions in your city. Write down names as they appear in those articles, along with the person's interests and involvements in other organizations.

One fund raiser stated that a very good contact to have in any city is the editor of the local newspaper's social page. In Houston, for example, the person who fits that recommendation is Betty

Ewing. She, for many years, has written the social column for the *Houston Chronicle* and probably knows more details about the Texas rich than anyone. Many other communities have their own version of Betty Ewing, who can tell you much of what you need to know about socially prominent city residents.

Think about your community. How has it changed recently? What big developments have taken place in real estate? Who were the developers? Chances are those persons have accumulated quite a lot of money in recent years. They might be interested in hearing about your upcoming building fund. What about asking that person to head up the committee to raise funds for that drive or at least to be a consultant to your building committee? The person, or the firm, should be listed in directories of the local Chamber of Commerce or the Board of Trade.

You might also check the *Who's Who in Real Estate*. It includes 12,000 persons from around the country who are appraisers, architects, brokers, developers and publishers of real estate related works. It includes regional indexing, so see which developers from your area are listed.

Gathering names for your potential major donor list is an ongoing process. You'll never finish adding to it. No matter where you are, write down names as they are mentioned to you, or as you think of a person who might be of help to you. Make a file of "potentials" and stuff it with any tidbits of information which you may need later. If one of those very-high-salaried business executives listed in the annual "highest paid" issue of *Business Week* and *Forbes* lives in your city, or happens to be interested in your cause, clip the article and stuff it into your file. At this initial point you may file everything together. Only when you begin to gather specific information on a person definitely identified as a potential donor will you need to make a folder for that individual. One organization has a file just labeled "Millionaires" for this random information.

A development officer from a small liberal arts college in the Midwest reported that an elderly scientist used to give $100 each year to his alma mater, but he seemed to very much enjoy the annual telephone conversation with the college official. Conversations went on, year after year, with the same $100 check coming in. After the man's death, it was revealed he had left the college $280,000. The conversations definitely had helped, but probably no amount of biographical background searching on this man would have brought earlier pleasant results. As Rockefeller said, each person must be approached differently and, as all fund raisers know, the unexpected sometimes happens regardless of methods used.

After you have your list, with key candidates noted, it is time to search for biographical information by whatever methods are available. This may be challenging. Often those with the most wealth are reluctant to tell others about themselves. Unlike much of the rest of the population, their egos do not need to be stroked by being listed in some of the "who's who" type books. Indeed, they prefer not to be listed in them.

When *Forbes* magazine made their listing of the country's most wealthy persons in the September 13, 1982, issue they based their list on information gathered by *Forbes* reporters. They admit it was not an easy task to figure out who were the richest and how they got that way.

In an introduction to that first "richest list" Harold Seneker stated, "Drawing up this list of America's richest people was . . . a formidable task. A majority of the people on it would have preferred not to have been listed." Seneker continued, "During the Age of Moguls, roughly from the Civil War to the Great Depression, the very rich came out of the closet and visibly enjoyed their wealth. But now, by and large, they have gone underground with it." Seneker said, however, that "Philanthropy is 'in' among the very wealthy," and all development officers can hope this is true.

The information on each of the 400 given in *Forbes* is about the same as that which you will want to know about any potential donor. It tells how much money the individual or family has, how they got it, and what they do with it. At least, it tells all that the reporters could unearth with little cooperation from those listed.

Shortly after the second "richest" listing in *Forbes* came out, several persons came to, or called, the public library to ask if we had mailing addresses for all 400 names identified by *Forbes*. We didn't, but I did invite the callers to come to the library where we would help find as many addresses as possible. One ardent searcher was either a somewhat naive fund raiser or a student trying to get through school with help from a rich donor; he spent days and days in the library carefully taking down names and addresses of the super-rich.

All that we could suggest, in his case, was that he start at the beginning of the list, using reference tools I will discuss later. Although you might guess that all of the wealthiest would be listed in *Who's Who in America* or other such publications, many are not. There is also a book with a title which promises more than it delivers. It is *How to Locate Anyone Who's Anyone*. It works better for rock and movie stars than it does for business executives or persons with family fortunes. A new version of that same type of book is *The Address Book,* a listing of 3,500 addresses of the famous. If Michael Jackson is on your potential donor list, you can find his address here, but don't look for an address for that wealthy, but non-flamboyant, widow down the street.

To show that many wealthy persons just aren't listed in many standard biographical reference books, I conducted an experiment at the District of Columbia Public Library where I work.

In the July 21, 1983 issue of the *Washington Post* an article mentioned a report from *Fortune* listing those who had increased their personal wealth in corporate shares by more than $100 million between August 12, 1982 and July 1, 1983. I checked this list against the *Marquis Index to All Books* and found that about a third were not listed in any Marquis publication. Some of those were the "invisible wealthy" who had made their fortune recently with computers, some were names of inherited-wealth families such as the Gettys.

These examples indicate the difficulty of finding the information you are seeking on rich persons. Even if your donors do not fall into the top 400, and most won't, many other persons of wealth prefer to protect their privacy. And, if it is hard to find information on the family breadwinner or person who made the fortune, it is twice as hard to find information on the spouse. In most cases this is the wife, and even though she may be very active in civic and community affairs, she may be almost invisible in published works unless she is prominent in a career of her own. As the husband is often sought to chair boards and committees, so is his wife. The name of Mrs. So and So looks about as good as that of the Mr. So and So on an organization's letterhead.

You should realize that, in the area of major philanthropy, the husband and the wife usually discuss together their major contribution to any organization. Involving the wife in your initial discussion about a gift can be a very good idea. Gather information about both the husband and wife before meeting the prospective donors. Often it is the wife who outlives the husband and becomes the one who will make important decisions on the family fortune.

Do not be discouraged by my caution that finding information on wealthy persons and their spouses may be difficult. If information on the "invisible rich" can be found, this book will give you the methods to do it. At first the search may seem cumbersome. After you have searched a few names with some success, you will know what sources work best for you and for the type of people on your prospects list.

While compiling donor lists, the question of whether to use packaged mailing lists comes up. This whole area of mailing list use by organizations has been adequately handled by many basic fund-raising books. Whether or not an organization chooses to use this technique depends on the organization's needs. The science, and it is surely that, has become very detailed. Everyone over the age of two must now be on someone's list which has been purchased by someone else to solicit contributions. For purposes of this book, using mailing lists will not be very helpful. These lists may bring in many "small bucks" but not the "mega bucks" we're talking about.

Before you discount the lists completely, you should know that lists of "wealthy Americans" can be purchased. One mailing list catalog which I saw recently put under that category persons who had ordered by mail books on stress, graduates of military schools, and donors to animal shelters! I doubt if these are completely accurate gauges.

It is possible, though, to get lists of Americans who own yachts, belong to impressive professional and social groups, have Rolls Royce automobiles, and give large amounts to charitable organizations similar to yours. These may be more helpful. Names on the lists can be received by region, state, city, or even by neighborhood Zip code, and they are available on glued labels. Probably the best advice about using mailing lists is to seek the help of a professional mailing broker or mailing service. Swapping, or selling, your own list may be desirable. This is surely telling you nothing you don't already know, if I can judge by the amount of contribution letters coming to even non-rich contributors.

Fund raisers may wish to contact one or both of the following associations for mailing list professionals: the National Council of Mailing List Brokers, 55 West 42nd Street, New York, NY 10001; or the Mailing List Brokers Professional Association, 663 Fifth Avenue, New York, NY 10022.

Also, the Women's Information Exchange, 1195 Valencia Street, San Francisco, CA 94110, supplies mailing lists on labels in Zip code order. These can be selected by women's organizations or by demographics and interests of individual women. Lists are created from a database of 10,000 women's organizations and 35,000 individual women.

*Direct Mail List Rates and Data* is published quarterly by Standard Data Service, Inc. This is the standard list selection and ordering tool used by direct mail professionals. It provides information on approximately 50,000 mailing lists.

The October 1, 1984 *Forbes* "richest" issue reports how information from marketers can be matched with Census Bureau data and Zip codes to determine where the nation's most wealthy live. A company, Claritas, Inc. in suburban Washington, D.C., uses such things as mailing lists from high-priced jewelry store catalogs, highbrow-magazine subscriptions, and warranty cards returned for appliances and automobiles to pinpoint rich persons. The company has determined that 4% of the nation's Zip codes concentrate about half the estimated 10,200 people who will make a million dollars this year, and half the households with assets of $1 million or more. Claritas predicts the lifestyles and buying habits of the rich. For a price Claritas will tell you who they are and where they live. $5,000 will give you a one-shot targeting; $100,000 will buy a permanent hookup. Customers, such as bank trust department officers, ask for listings according to degrees of wealth.

Other companies, perhaps in your area, do this same type of thing. You can also do it yourself on a less professional scale. You can find your city's richest by using a Zip code map along with city real estate and *Haines Criss-Cross Directories*. Your list won't have the precision of a Claritas list, but it will be a lot less expensive! You can guess where the richest Zip codes are with a little investigation, then compile your lists from those areas.

Another useful locator is a publication called *Congressional District Zip Codes* which is a cross-reference index to the nation's 40,000 Zip codes in all congressional districts. The primary use of this book is by associations, lobbyists and others who wish to influence a particular member of Congress. Fund raisers, particularly political fund raisers, must use this same source to solicit campaign contributions. So can your organization. Statistical data is gathered from this set, still using Zip codes, to determine what is going on in congressional districts.

Very specialized lists can be used to give names of wealthy individuals which may be interested in your field. If you are a struggling theater group, it may be of help to know there is a publication called *Angels* which lists thousands of investors in theatrical and motion picture productions nationwide. Names, addresses and amount invested are given. One, just one, angel may be all that you need. The publication costs $150. Angels do not come cheaply in today's world, it seems, and neither does information about them.

# 5
# What Information Do You Need?

*How you got it, that is the question;*
*whether by right or by wrong.*

*Plautus c. 200 B.C.*

*C*all it whatever you want, the basis of any organization's donor list should be a Personal Data Sheet on each actual or potential major donor. As well as summarizing past donations or contacts, the sheet should contain as much biographical information as can be obtained from whatever sources. To begin a sheet, you may have nothing more than a name and some indication of where you heard of the person.

Information on this data sheet can be obtained verbally from those who know the person, or from printed sources. Keep track of the reference source for each item of information, if possible, and note the date when the information was obtained.

An example of how this information is gathered and used by trustees and development officers was given by Amy Cunningham in *Washingtonian*, December, 1982. This article on fundraising techniques of major Washington charities told how the National Gallery searches for 20th-century Medicis to make the great museum ever greater.

> How do gallery trustees and . . . committee members cultivate their sources and get people to give? First, all correspondence and contact with the millionaire in question is laboriously documented in a file. Did he come to Patron's Day? What did he say at the Collectors Committee meeting? Has he suggested meeting a trustee for lunch? Then an extensive biography is compiled from magazine articles, newspaper clips, and recollections of the man as reported to the development office by trustees. Where did the potential donor go to graduate school? What is his wife's name? And, most important, what is his history of giving? Does he donate large sums of money only to the arts? What are his current financial commitments? The National Gallery has him pegged down to his tie clip right there in the file.

That, in a nutshell, is the type of information you will want to compile for each of your potential large donors. Jerold Panas, in *Mega Gifts, Who Gives Them, Who Gets Them*, writes, "Research your prospect with finite care and painstaking attention. No detail is too small. What might appear to be an insignificant bit of information can often open the door to the mega gift."

Even though you will want to make your Personal Data Sheet reflect your organization, you may wish to consider gathering the following information.

---

### Personal Data Sheet:

NAME:
List the principal donor's complete name. List the spouse's name. List maiden names for married women.

ADDRESS:
List both office and home addresses, with phone numbers. Is there a different summer (or winter) address? List it.

PROFESSION:
List as much information as possible about the person's main profession or source of income. List position title and a history of the person's connection with the firm or organization. Is the company known for its contributions to charity? (This person may be responsible.)

PROFESSIONAL POSITIONS:
List here directorships on other companies, connections with local or national professional organizations, and memberships on national or local commissions or task forces.

CLUBS AND ORGANIZATIONS:
Include here social as well as non-profit and community organizations. Is the person an officer or on the board of any of these? What clubs does he or she belong to? What are the requirements for club membership? Is achievement in a particular field necessary? Is he or she a member of golf or other sport clubs?

PERSONAL HISTORY:
Here it is possible to mention even far-fetched tidbits of information. Is the person an avid bird-watcher, a motorcycle racer, interested in sailing, a player of Medieval music, interested in high school hockey, fond of Early American crafts, or known to be a gourmet cook? Write down anything which may make a topic of conversation during the first meeting with a member of the board or development officer.

FINANCIAL POSITION:
List here as much information as you can possibly find out through some of the sources which will be discussed later. Knowing the range of wealth will make it easier for you to suggest a possible donation. Give annual salary, or an estimate of that. Give major real estate or stock holdings. Where did the family wealth originate? Was much of it inherited? Has the family been thought of in your community as one which contributes generously to charities? What are the person's or family's major contributions to organizations?

AFFILIATION WITH YOUR ORGANIZATION:
This is perhaps the most useful part of the Personal Data Sheet. It tells why this person should be interested in your organization or its cause. Is the donor an alumnus or an alumna of your school, the parent of a student? Does he or she live in the neighborhood? Has a

child been a patient at your hospital? Has he or she had a history of supporting musical organizations? Be creative. List as many reasons as you can think of why this persons should support your organization, institution, or political party.

PREPARED BY:
Put down the person or persons who compiled this information.

DATE:
Date material as it is added to the file.

---

Individual organizations such as yours may wish to tailor the date sheet to reflect your particular needs. Add any items to the sheet which you think would help your development officers. Update the information at regular intervals. For example, every two years when a new edition of *Who's Who in America* is published, you might wish to check it for changes in employment or membership on boards or commissions. Update the addresses as you find new information. Volunteers may be used to gather basic information.

Information gathered for this file should be considered confidential, for office use only.

Make a file for each prospective or active major donor. Add to that file the Personal Data Sheet, newspaper and periodical clippings, and all correspondence or records of contact with the person. New staff in your development office should be able to pick up a file and have a complete history of this person's affiliation with your group.

Some institutions color code the donor file, using a separate color for each category of givers. Use whatever method works best for you. There are books on management of non-profit organizations which suggest guidelines for setting up and maintaining your office procedures. One of these which gives information on setting up both corporate and individual donor files is *Prospecting: Searching Out the Philanthropic Dollar* by James K.

Hickey and Elizabeth Koochoo.

The pages following will indicate sources for the information needed on the Personal Data Sheet. One word of caution. You may have to leave many blank spaces on this sheet. Ideally, you would like to have all that information; realistically, you may not be able to fill in all the blanks. Some of the information is just not available, regardless of your skill in searching through all of the suggested sources.

And, as already mentioned, if it is hard to find information on the principal donor or the family's principal money-maker, it is much more difficult to find information on that person's spouse. Wives of rich men are often asked to serve on boards or to act as chairpersons for many types of functions, but personal information on them is often scant. Nevertheless, fill in as much information on the wife as you find when researching her husband. She may also have a lot to say about family contributions.

Even though potential donors of large amounts must know that they will be researched by organizations, it is wise not to make an issue that this information gathering is going on behind the scenes.

# 6

# Where to Find Biographical Information in Books

*When Mae West found out that she wasn't
in the big red Who's Who in America book,
she cooed coolly, "Well, the old boy who publishes that
isn't in my little black book either."*

Armed with your list of potential donors, your first stop should be the local public library. You may, of course, have to go other places as well for information, but you will be amazed at the library's variety of sources on wealthy persons. If yours is a large city public library, most of what you need will be right there. If the library is small, it will probably be part of a state or regional library system and resources in that larger area can be made available to you. If what you need is not available locally, ask your librarian how to pursue your search at a larger facility. Some states and areas do a better job of library networking than others.

When you enter the library, ask where biographical reference books are kept. Some libraries have a biography section. Many do not, but still keep biographical information together. If the library uses the Dewey Decimal System of cataloging, most of the books you need will be classed in the 920 section. If the Library of Congress Cataloging System is used, the books will be arranged according to specific subject areas (e.g., biographical books on scientists will be with other books on science).

Don't be reluctant about asking a librarian for help. That is precisely what he or she is there for! Nothing is more frustrating for a librarian than to have library users go away without the desired information because the person failed to ask for what they did not find by themselves. The librarian is your guide, assume that he or she knows more about how to find information than you do. After all, you know more about fund raising than the librarian.

You don't have to tell the librarian why you want the information, or even the name of the person being researched, but give the librarian some clues if you have them. Is the person living or dead? (I know, deceased persons do not write checks, but their descendents do.) Is the person from this city or where? What professional group is the person in? If you know the answers to those questions, it will make the search easier, if you don't, ask anyway. Sometimes it is useful for the librarian to know where you heard of this person. It's all a bit like a treasure hunt. Each clue brings you closer to the pot of gold. A missed clue might result in an impasse.

One thing to remember about public libraries: most of them offer telephone reference services. Although lengthy research cannot be done for you over the phone, the library can often tell you what materials exist on the name you seek. An entry from a who's who type book can usually be read to you over the phone, although you may wish to go in to photocopy the entry for your own file. Sometimes the librarian's answer will be, "Nothing has been found on that name in the few minutes I have looked, but please come in and we will help you search further." Don't expect the librarian to do all of your research for you, but do expect help. Use the professional librarian's expertise.

Here are some titles which you will find most useful. Complete bibliographical information on these biographical sources is given at the end of this book. Most librarians will recognize these books by their titles.

The most useful book for your research will probably by *Who's Who in America (WWA)*. Information given in *WWA* includes, in most cases, the following: complete name, birthdate and place, education, publications, activities, marital status, family names, home and office addresses, career history, memberships, military record, religion and political affiliation. Some include a short statement called, "Thoughts on My Life."

The typical *Who's Who in America* entry gives quite a good account of a person. It tells how the person got where he or she is now, and what organizations the person is interested in outside of professional concerns. The British *Who's Who* sometimes adds a bit of zip in their entries, whereas the American version never comes up with anything very tantalizing about the biographees. The British version lists hobbies and I sometimes wish the American one would also. A recent obituary for a British Lord quoted the *Who's Who* as listing the man's hobby as "kicking pigeons." Some persons are listed in *WWA* because of their current position as congresspersons, ambassadors, top political and government figures, and such. Others are listed because of outstanding achievement in a particular field. Each biographee is given the opportunity to update and proofread all information. If they do not return the form, *WWA* editors add an asterisk after the entry. If an asterisk follows an entry you may wish to look elsewhere — for a current address, for example.

If you can purchase one source, this is probably the one you will want to buy. The 1984-1985 edition, the 43rd, costs $135 and contains 74,000 biographees. Don't be surprised, though, if the person you are looking for is not among them. For instance, one former editor of *WWA*, asked why some people get in and some don't, replied that he himself wasn't in it, but his sister was. It probably mattered that his sister is Beverly Sills.

Keep in mind that people, even those who were once listed, may not be listed forever. After retirement, or after leaving a position which gets one automatically listed, the name is often dropped. If you think your person may have been more prominent years ago, ask to see back editions of *WWA*. Most larger public libraries keep these old volumes.

Marquis Who's Who, Inc. also puts out many other biographical sources which will be useful in any donor search. Some are for particular professions, others are by regions of the country, and there is a separate *Who's Who of American Women*.

Regional volumes are *Who's Who in the East, Who's Who in the West, Who's Who in the Midwest,* and *Who's Who in the South and Southwest.* Marquis publishes many professional volumes. Of these, the ones most useful to development officers are *Who's Who in American Law, Who's Who in Religion, Who's Who in Finance and Industry* and *Directory of Medical Specialists. Who's Who in the World* also includes many prominent Americans.

Since 1974 Marquis has been publishing annual indexes to all of their publications, making it possible to check only one book for listings in all current editions of the above mentioned books. That index is now in two volumes. Volume One is an alphabetical listing of more than 260,000 profiles. Volume Two is divided geographically by country, state and city. This feature will make it possible for you to identify "who's who" persons in your locality. You can check the complete entry in the indicated volume for more information on the biographee.

In 1982 Marquis did a *Professional/Geographical Index* which enables searchers to find people in their area who were classified by profession. This index covers only those in *WWA*, not the regional or other publications. Professional categories include art, business, education, government, law, medicine, religion, sports, science and technology. The volume is divided into country, state and city; then into professional categories.

These indexes are made possible by the wonders of computer publishing. There is no end to the possibilities of accessing the information in biographical directories. There is even a *Birthdate Index to WWA*. I wasn't sure how fund raisers could benefit from this new source of information until I read that the noted philanthropist Dr. Armand Hammer had doubled his initial foundation gift to the National Symphony after Washington's Mayor Marion Barry had declared Hammer's birthday "Dr. Armand Hammer Day" at a symphony concert. Using this index may be worth considering. At least, you could send birthday cards to all those on your donor list who are listed in *WWA*! Names are listed under each day of the year along with current occupation, preferred mailing address, and year of birth. Check to see whose birthday is coming up, then let your imagination go wild. Send a birthday card to your Senator, remember your doctor on that important day, send balloons to your local millionaire, have a cake delivered to the company executive on the *Business Week* "highest paid" list (it may be lonely at the top). And be sure to include a donor contribution envelope with each birthday card! It may be worth $59 to buy the *Birthdate Index* so you can refer to it each morning to see who has a birthday that day.

Another index, which may be more useful, is the *Directory of*

*Women in Marquis Who's Who Publications,* published in 1983. It picks out women from all of the publications, not just *WWA*. Women may be located by name or by geographical location. With each name is an occupational description, address and location symbol to the volume which contains the original entry. I can see this volume being very useful to development officers for organizations which look to women for major contributions and support.

College and university development officers should be aware that the computers of Marquis have now identified *WWA* biographees and listed them with their alma mater. This will identify the "highest-achieving alumni" (or at least those high-achievers who are listed in *WWA*) and make it possible to know where to find your elusive graduates. Look for *Who's Who in America College Alumni Directory,* published in 1983. Here, under the college name, is the person's name, a brief occupational description and an up-to-date home or office address. Marquis' catalog states this is "an essential resource for alumni offices, special events coordinators, public relations departments, and honorary award committees. It opens opportunities to give due recognition to those who reflect the success of your school. It lets you access the knowledge, talent, and resources of this distinguished group." The directory was published at the astonishing cost of $375 (to pay for the computer, no doubt), but it has now been discounted. If it sounds useful to you, call Marquis for a current price. Their order number is 1-800-428-3898.

With this possible exception, most of the many Marquis publications will be available at your public library. Some fund-raising offices need to have their own *Who's Who in America* because it is used so often. Others purchase just the *Index to All Books* which will then serve as a locator tool. Identifying who is listed where makes it easier to get the information with a visit or a call to the library. Others purchase the regional volume which covers their area. The two-volume *Index* costs about $70; each regional volume is about $85.

*Who's Who in America* is now available on-line through DIALOG Information Services. More information on computer searching will come later in this book.

This classic reference book, *Who's Who in America,* which is consulted in most libraries second only to dictionaries, has been published since 1899 (when it came out as the American equivalent of the earlier *Who's Who* published in London). As you can imagine, there are many imitators which attempt to latch on to the status connected with being listed in *WWA.* The object of these other publications is to sound as much like *WWA* as possible, but to be different enough so they will not be sued by Marquis. The dozens of spurious who's who publications which come out each year will probably be of little use to the fund raiser. Most of these books are designed to stroke the ego of those listed. In many cases, it is the billfold which is stroked, as the cost of inclusion is often the cost of the published book. Your wealthy donors do not need this type of vanity-stroking and you will seldom find their names in these books.

Recently, with some fanfare, an unknown publisher "out by the Beltway" announced a *Who's Who in Washington.* Although we who work in Washington would have welcomed a good local publication of notable persons, this surely was not that. How can a librarian trust a book which puts The National Symphony under The? Ask your local librarian if there is a similar book for your city, but don't be surprised if the names you seek aren't in it. Also, beware of biographical books which have adjectives in their title: books listing persons who are "outstanding," "prominent," or "distinguished." They are probably vanity publications.

Most individual states do not have a reliable biographical tool for that state. During the 1976 Bicentennial celebration many persons were solicited to be in state who's who books. As far as I can tell, even those which were actually published were not very helpful. One brochure indicated that having your name entered in a particular book would indicate that you were alive in 1976. It hardly seems a noteworthy achievement.

You may be disappointed if the names you seek are not in one of the many Marquis publications, but do not be surprised. You may have to look further for information and, even if the person is listed there, you may wish for more personal information than is available in Marquis. Even though current editions of the Marquis publications include over 260,000 persons, they may not include the one name you need. Luckily, there are many other possibilities for finding information.

Another index lists 3,200,000 persons. It is an index to 350 current and retrospective biographical dictionaries. Your names may be listed there. This is the *Biography and Genealogy Master Index (BGMI)* published by Gale Research Company as part of the Gale Biographical Index Series. This second edition is an eight-volume set published in 1980. Some libraries will have an earlier edition called the *Biographical Dictionaries Master Index*, published in 1975 with supplements since then. As part of this same series, there are several individual volumes which index persons by categories such as authors, performers and such. An historical index will be described later.

Whereas the Marquis index lists only persons in that company's publication, the Gale index lists many, many different sources. Among those listed are the Marquis publications. Because this Gale publication puts so many different types of books in one index, listing both living and deceased persons together, I find that the Marquis index is a better tool to begin with. On the other hand, you may also need the Gale index because of the large numbers of names indexed there. Many of the non-Marquis biographical directories which will be mentioned later are indexed in *BGMI*.

Some of the reference works indexed in these master indexes give only minimal information about a person. Others give extensive accounts of a person's life. An example of the first category would be a reference to an association membership directory where not much more than a person's name and professional affiliation is given.

At the other end. *Current Biography* is an example of a resource giving a lot of personal information. This set of books, which began publication in 1940, gives detailed information about persons who were prominent in many areas or professions at the time the entry appeared. In the years since its beginning, *Current Biography* has covered 300-350 persons each year, so well over

13,000 persons have been profiled.

Each article gives full name (and original name, if different), parents and family information, educational background, professional development, and reasons for being newsworthy. The entries are written in narrative style with the biographee's personality explored in the article. Often quotations by the person are given. A bibliography for further information follows each entry.

*Current Biography* is published monthly in paper format, then compiled into an annual volume. Entries in the complete set can be checked by consulting four indexes, the *Current Biography Cumulated Index 1940-1970*, the 1980 annual volume, the latest bound volume after 1980, and the last paperback monthly issue. Each annual volume has a profession index, and philanthropists are listed as such.

If your searched-for person is well enough known to be in *Current Biography*, your search can probably be concluded. Most people, no matter how wealthy, won't make it into *Current Biography*. However, it does include a good cross-section of personalities.

Many wealthy Americans are also listed in the *International Who's Who*. Americans listed there often have international reputations and may, for example, be international businesspeople or involved in international organizations or foreign diplomacy.

There are, of course, many other biographical reference books. Most of those contain persons in a particular profession or category. Many will be discussed later.

# 7

# Where to Find Biographical Information in Other Sources

*Someone once referred to a foundation
as a body of money completely surrounded
by people who want some.*

For additional information about those located in a who's who type directory, and those not yet located, it is a good idea to consult magazine indexes to see if there has been an article written about them. The comings and goings of wealthy persons are often better documented than the lives of the ordinary person. An index to periodicals will lead you to that documentation.

*Readers' Guide to Periodical Literature* has been around the longest and is found in even the smallest of libraries. It is published twice a month (monthly in July and August) with frequent cumulations and, finally, bound volumes. Magazines indexed tend to be of national interest and accessibility. As this index has been published since 1900, there is much historical information to be found here. If you are looking for the history of an especially

51

prominent family, you should look into older volumes for articles. If there were significant events for that family, check the years when the events happened for the most coverage. Check under the individual or family name. Many libraries take all the periodicals indexed in *Readers' Guide,* and many keep all back issues either in bound volumes or on microfilm. You should have no trouble finding the actual article after you find the citation.

A new guide, begun in the late 1970s, is *Magazine Index.* This is a reel of microfilm which brings together about five years of periodical citations in one alphabetical cumulation. It is provided to libraries in its own easy-to-use microfilm reader, with a new reel replacing the old one each month. Since it indexes more than twice as many periodicals as *Readers' Guide,* it includes many local publications which may have the names you need. Examples of city magazines with lots of coverage of the "beautiful people" are *Los Angeles, New Orleans, Chicago, Philadelphia,* and *Washingtonian.* If your city magazine is indexed in *Magazine Index,* you may be in luck in your search by using this reference tool.

*Access: The Supplementary Index to Periodicals* indexes over 300 magazines but does not duplicate any covered by *Readers' Guide.* Because of this, *Access* is also very good for city and regional magazines. It comes out three times a year with an annual cumulation.

There are many magazines which cover the lives of rich persons. *Town and Country* and *Vogue* are just two examples. By using a magazine index you have access to any articles written about persons on your donor list. Don't neglect this possibility.

Aside from finding individual names in the indexes, you may also use this method to find general articles about lifestyles of the wealthy, and to find names of wealthy persons who might be useful to your organization. Some subject headings which may be helpful are these: Capitalists and Financiers - Biography; Children of the Rich; Leisure Class; Millionaires; Millionairesses; Wealth-Case Studies; and Philanthropy.

A quick check under these topics produced titles such as "New Millionaires," "Seven Who've Made It Big," "Moneymakers of the 80s," and "Top Black Money Makers." There are a lot more, and many articles not only give the names of the rich but also short biographical sketches. *Town and Country,* as mentioned previously, named the Texans with $30 million and over in its September 1979 issue. All the fund raisers in Texas probably photocopied that article.

Another guide to biographical information in published sources is *Biography Index* which covers both periodicals and books of collective biography. It works like *Readers' Guide,* with annual and triennial volumes. Its professional index to articles is also useful. Because this indexes books of collective biography as well as periodicals, you might pick up some additional names from those books.

For business people, the best source of information from periodical literature is *Business Index.* This is published by the same company, in the same microfilm format, as *Magazine Index.* It indexes virtually all of the business-related magazines and newspapers in the country. Many, many names and company names are listed. Here too it is wise to check under some of the before-mentioned topics for interesting articles on the rich. About five years cumulation for 813 periodicals is available in one alphabetical listing.

Comparable to *Readers' Guide,* and from the same company, is *Business Periodicals Index.* As this has been published since 1958, it is well worth checking the bound volumes for published articles before the microfilmed *Business Index* was begun.

Of the 520,000 millionaires (or just plain wealthy persons) in this country, many, or most, will not be featured in periodical articles. For everyone who gives splashy parties or is seen at all the right sunny resorts, there is the quiet widow living modestly somewhere in the Midwest on a fortune her husband left following years of wise investments. She will be listed in none of the biographical directories mentioned so far, nor will she be the subject of an article in *Town and Country.* She may, however, have been written up in her local newspaper because of her collection of Early American quilts. Her husband's obituary probably made the state's biggest newspaper. With a little luck and some perseverance you can find those articles. You will need to consult newspaper indexes.

The most useful newspaper indexes will be the ones which index the newspapers in your area, if that is where your major donors live. Many newspapers, however, are not indexed. If there is an index, you can be very sure that the public library will have it. If there is no printed index for your newspaper, ask at the library if there is an "in-house" index to the paper. Many local-history rooms of public libraries have done some of their own indexing and clipping for years. Often the articles receiving this attention have been on prominent families. This same type of selective indexing and clipping may also have been done by local historical societies. Call that society and ask if they have newspaper-clipping files for your use. If they went to the trouble of gathering the material, they will be happy to have someone use it. Ask too if there is an index to the historical society papers which are published in many cities.

In most libraries the files will be by family name. Occasionally, however, there may be general categories such as "millionaires," "businesses," or even "politicians." You may strike it lucky and find just the article you need in one of those files.

If the prominent or wealthy person about whom you seek information is in a distant city, you can write to that public library and ask if a file exists on that person. If it does, ask that the materials be photocopied for you. You will be charged a fee, but it is quite inexpensive, probably less than a long-distance phone call for information. And you have the copied articles for your own file. Sometimes, depending on the size of the library staff and the availability of adequate indexing, more extensive help can be given. For example, some libraries will check an index for newspaper articles and make a copy from the microfilm for you. If you know the date of an obituary for instance, you can probably get a copy from the public library of the city where the person lived at the time of death. Don't expect the librarians to do extensive research for you; but also don't discount the possibility of getting what you want by mail. The search may be less complicated than you think and easily done by a public librarian.

Besides the use of newspaper indexes to find information, keep in mind that many libraries have clipping files. Besides those mentioned in the local-history room, there are files in other parts of a library. If there is a biography division, ask there for help. If you vaguely remember reading about the person in the local paper five (or was it six?) years ago, mention that possibility. Don't worry that you don't know the date of the article. These vertical files are sometimes treasure troves for fund raisers. Clippings and articles kept there may go back decades, especially if the library is an old one, and may document the wealthy families in the city. If there are family articles there, they may answer many of your questions.

Recently, a library patron was looking for the relationship between a prominent architect and a very well-known, wealthy family. The architect went by her married name, but the patron thought she was from that other family. In our file on the family we found a *Time* article on an event in the family which gave a complete family tree. The question was answered.

Aside from these indexes and clipping files, there is a wealth of information available in almost every community. Unfortunately, in some cases, it is not very accessible. Most newspaper libraries or "morgues" are not open to the public even though they often have wonderful back files on individuals, families and local companies—just what a fund raiser needs. If you think the newspaper library might have what you need, give it a try. Ask the newspaper librarians if they can be of any help to you. They may be able to tell you the date of an article which you can then find elsewhere. They may suggest other ways to help you also.

These libraries are specifically designed to be of help to current newspaper staff. Although a survey done by Inland Daily Press Association revealed that two-thirds of libraries at newspapers allowed some public access to their materials, the reality is probably that they will refer most public inquiries to the local public library where complete back files of the newspaper are held.

Sometimes these newspaper morgues, virtual gold mines of information on prominent families, do become open to the public. This rather recent development is the result of many newspapers going out of business. The newspaper library is then given to another institution where it is opened for general use.

One example is the *Washington Star* which, after over 100 years of publication, suddenly closed its doors in 1981. The rival *Washington Post* bought the building owned by the *Star* and got the library also. As the *Post* had no need for this morgue, it was given to the District of Columbia Public Library, for the local-history collection. As the *Star* had always been considered the main newspaper for local news, it had great files on individuals in Washington. Looking for information on rich Washington families is now much easier than it was before the *Star* library became public property.

In Philadelphia, the *Evening Bulletin* ceased publication in January, 1982. Its library, dating back 134 years, has been donated to the Temple University Paley Library. It contains ten million clippings! It is a certainty that the prominent, and probably the wealthy, citizens of Philadelphia are well-documented in that massive clipping file.

The morgue of the *New York Sun* is in the New York Public Library; the *Newark News* is at the Newark Public Library and the Brooklyn Library has the morgue of the *Brooklyn Eagle*. The *Cleveland Press* morgue went to the Cleveland State University. The *St. Paul Pioneer Press-Dispatch* has given many older clips to the Minnesota Historical Society, and the *San Francisco Chronicle* is planning to give its morgue to the California Historical Society. Some morgues have met less pleasant fates. Many have been warehoused, or worse, have become landfill.

If a major newspaper in your area has recently stopped publication, ask around and find out what happened to the newspaper morgue. It may be available for your use.

Next to your own community newspaper, the most useful newspaper index will be a national one such as the index to the *New York Times*. Fortunately, that newspaper is well-documented. The founders of the *Times* in 1851 envisioned the newspaper as an historical record, and thus required that an index be kept to it. The indexing was done by other publishers until 1913 when the newspaper started to publish its own index. It exists in semi-annual compilations from 1913 to 1930, with annual compilations thereafter. Currently it is published bimonthly, with quarterly and annual cumulations. Many public libraries of any size have this index, as well as the newspaper itself, on microfilm.

In 1976 a useful set of 22 volumes was published by a different company as a further index to the *Times*. Called *The Personal Name Index*, it provides name citations to the *New York Times Index*, not to the actual newspaper. By picking up individual names from all of the volumes between 1851 and 1974, it puts into one alphabetical order all names indexed during those years. Later years are in supplements. Because this set of books is very expensive, many public libraries will not have this reference tool.

One good way to find biographical information in the *New York Times* is to guess the year or series of years in which a person was well-known and then zero in on that period by checking the appropriate annual indexes. For example, you may be looking for a person who is now retired, but who was politically prominent 20 years ago. Skip the years in between and concentrate on those most active years of your person.

Another tool which is often available in local libraries is the index to the *Wall Street Journal*. Libraries which have the *Journal* on microfilm will usually also have this index, which began in 1958. For individual names, as well as for names of corporations and their histories, this is extremely useful. This index is divided into two parts: corporate news and general news. It contains a special section for personalities and obituaries of prominent persons.

During the early 1970s many other newspapers were indexed by Bell and Howell. Besides doing several major city newspapers, they also continued indexing the *Christian Science Monitor*, which had done its own index from 1960 to 1979.

The *Washington Post* was indexed by Bell and Howell beginning in 1971. In 1979 Research Publications Inc. began the *Official Washington Post Index* with monthly issues and an annual cumulation.

The *National Newspaper Index* straddles the fence between the modern computer and the old-fashioned printed index. This microfilm indexes the *Christian Science Monitor*, the *New York*

*Times,* the *Los Angeles Times,* the *Wall Street Journal,* and the *Washington Post.* Although it is available through DIALOG, it is most often used in its microfilm form and is available in many libraries.

While there are many possibilities for newspaper indexes, it is best to ask the library you plan to use what is available there either online, in print or on microfilm. Should you need to know if there is an index for a specific newspaper in a specific city, you can check in one of two guides to newspaper indexes. These tell which newspapers are indexed, and where the indexes are located. One is *Newspaper Indexes: A Location and Subject Guide for Researchers,* a three-volume set; the other is *Lathrop Report on Newspaper Indexes.* Aside from listing published indexes, these often tell of unpublished indexes which exist on cards or in clipping files. Use these with some caution. The accuracy of the first guide depended on librarians returning a questionnaire which sometimes did not happen. It may be safer just to write to the public library in the out-of-town locality where you are seeking information.

To find which are the major newspapers in other cities where you need to research individuals, consult the *Ayer Directory of Publications* available in most libraries. This geographical arrangement includes magazines as well as newspapers and has been published since 1880. Newspaper libraries are listed in the *Directory of Newspaper Libraries in the U.S. and Canada* put out by the Special Libraries Association.

While most newspaper indexes only direct you to the edition of the paper in which an article appeared, there is one service which includes the entire original article. It is the *New York Times Biographical Edition,* a compilation of current biographical information of general interest which began in 1970. (In 1969 the same service was in a slightly different format.) This loose-leaf service is published monthly and reprints actual biographical articles from the daily and Sunday editions of the *Times.* Not all obituaries are included, just those of fairly prominent persons who command some national interest. If your person is prominent, especially in the New York area, this service, available in many libraries, may have just what you need.

Because most libraries can't afford to subscribe to major newspapers from every state, there is a service which provides information on microfilm at a fraction of the cost of individual subscriptions. It offers material from about 200 newspapers in over 130 U.S. cities. It is *News Bank,* which clips articles, rearranges them, then microfilms the results. Articles are grouped into 13 topics, often according to national issues: also included is a "figures in the news " section.

The best way to find information on out-of-town newspapers is by online computer searching, discussed in Chapter 10. This may be one of the most effective methods you will use for up-to-date information.

Although it cannot be well-documented, word-of-mouth is one of the most useful "other sources" for finding information about the wealthy in any community. As social editors for newspapers often know who is in and who is out of the local social scene, so fund raisers soon pick up a feel for the big givers in their areas. There gets to be a sort of "insider information," not unlike that in stock market trading, about personal fortunes and the personal idiosyncrasies of the rich. This includes who's got the money and who's giving it away. When a rich person dies, fund raisers often know the beneficiaries by researching probated wills.

Since *Forbes* did its "richest" issue, now many city and regional newspapers and magazines are getting the same idea and are doing such a list of the rich for their areas. There is obvious interest in the subject, judging by the sales figures for the *Forbes* issue each fall.

It's just as hard, local researchers are finding, to discover the most wealthy in their own area as it was for *Forbes* to do for the entire country. Researchers must do the same type of digging. Putting the names on the list to be investigated, to see if they really belong there, often is done by a more or less haphazard method. In one city a magazine publisher sat down with his staff and brainstormed about the names for the list. Researchers then talked to fund raisers, among others, to get suggestions.

Just as fund raisers may have helped in many cities to form

such lists of the rich, so they will benefit when the lists are published. Although the information will be very speculative, it will be a beginning point which can lead to further research for fund raisers and development officers.

# 8

# How to Find Information on Persons in Specific Categories

*Rich gifts wax poor when
givers prove unkind.*

*Shakespeare*

Many of the potential donors on your list will be business people. There are many directories which give information about businesses, and some include biographical information about the corporate officers. Keep in mind that this information is useful in seeking the corporate donation as well as the individual donation. The before-mentioned Marquis publication *Who's Who in Finance and Industry* is a very useful source. The latest edition contains more than 21,000 key decision makers from banking, insurance, transportation, government regulatory agencies, major corporations and related fields. It follows the basic who's who format and is published biannually.

Along with that source, the other most useful set of books is *Standard and Poor's Register of Corporations, Directors and Executives*. Volume Two is the one which gives the biographical information you are looking for. Directors, presidents, chief executive officers, vice presidents and other executives are listed alphabetically. It gives the current principal business affiliation with titles, as well as other business and professional organizations with which the person is involved. Business and residence addresses are given. Personal information includes date and place of birth, education, and corporate and fraternal memberships. This is the most inclusive directory of business people.

Another source is *Dun and Bradstreet Million Dollar Directory*. It gives no biographical information on those in leadership positions in large companies, but it does identify who is where. Because there is a geographical listing, it is useful for picking out those companies in your area which fit into the category of million dollar businesses. Executives of these successful companies may become prime targets for contributions.

A source of regional information about businesses and business people is a series of business journals which, although affiliated, are published separately. The Cordovan Business Journals (recently bought out by Scripps Howard) publish separate journals in several areas and are geared to local business news for each area. Cities or regions which have these journals are Atlanta, Dallas/Fort Worth, Houston, Los Angeles, Phoenix, Puget Sound, Rocky Mountain, San Diego, San Francisco, South Florida and Washington, D.C. An example of a recent issue useful to fund raisers listed the top salaries or compensation paid executives by local companies, as well as those paid to top chief executive officers around the country. Weekly issues give major appointments to executive posts in local big businesses and major real estate transactions for the area.

*Contacts Influential* business directory is published in over 25 cities and areas in the United States. Listings in this set are by types of businesses in a metropolitan region, name of business, and location by Zip. Because the set has a listing of personal names, it is possible to identify someone who may not be listed in other business biographical books but who may be an executive of a local business. If there is a *Contacts Influential* published for your area, it will probably be leased to your public library. (Don't expect to photocopy the information you want from it. It is leased with a "no photocopying" clause which the company takes very seriously. Plan to spend an afternoon at the library with pen in hand.)

*Dun and Bradstreet Reference Book of Corporate Managements* includes companies with annual sales of $29 million and/or with 1,000 or more employees. It contains biographical information on directors and elected officials of about 2,400 companies. Basic biographical information along with career data is given, with officers listed under the company name. There is also an alphabetical index of company officers.

As there are so many business-related reference books, only those with at least some biographical information or those which can serve to identify a person with a particular company, are listed here. The best way to use the many business reference books is to throw yourself at the mercy of a good business librarian and let yourself be led to the most useful book for your purposes. In each geographical area there are directories of trade associations, marketing guides and similar works which should be consulted to find information on business people.

*Where to Find Business Information: A Worldwide Guide for Everyone Who Needs the Answer to Business Questions*, available in many libraries, may lead you to other business sources. Recently a development officer came to the library looking for a list of the 50 largest insurance companies with their chief executive officer. A combination of the *Fortune* magazine annual listing of non-industrial companies and the *Dun and Bradstreet Reference Book of Corporate Managements* answered the question.

One book, more interesting than really helpful, is *Everybody's Business: An Almanac*. The subtitle "The Irreverent Guide to Corporate America" indicates that it is a rather gossipy volume with a behind-the-scenes look at many companies. If the person you are researching works for one of those companies, it may be worth taking a look at the book to determine a "feel" for the company.

Should you know the names of companies with which your donors are affiliated, it is useful to see the companies' annual reports to get some idea of their type of business and their size. For finding salary information on the top officials, the best source is the proxy statement for the company, which includes information on the annual remuneration of top executives. These statements are sent to shareholders before the annual meeting and tell who are the officers and directors of the company. The statement also tells how many shares are held by those persons, and the age and principal occupations of those on the board.

Should the person you are researching be a member of the board of directors of Pan American World Airways, for example, you can find the person's age, the date he or she became a Pan Am director, the position on the board, other companies the person is affiliated with, and even the person's involvement on charitable, cultural and academic boards. Members of the Pan Am board, to continue to use that example, are interested in the Boy Scouts of America, Johns Hopkins University, the Philadelphia Museum of Art, the Wildlife Management Institute, the J. Paul Getty Trust, and a host of other organizations. If your organization resembles one of those, that particular board member may also be interested in hearing from you.

Background occupational information is given for directors, executives and nominees. More important, if you are making some determination about a prospect's wealth, the Pan Am proxy statement tells the person's stock ownership in that company, his cash compensation, and other pertinent financial information as it relates to Pan Am. Most other proxy statements follow this same pattern.

Many annual reports for local and national companies are available at the public library, in their business division. Brokerage houses can also supply annual reports. They don't have to know, when you request the report, that you are researching the company's vice president rather than considering a stock purchase.

The U.S. Securities and Exchange Commission (SEC) was

established in 1934 to protect the integrity of the business financing system. As such, the SEC requires public disclosure of pertinent data relating to all companies which are publicly owned. 10-K, 8-K or 13-D are documents which give information about the stock transactions of major stockholders or operations of a company. They are on file at SEC offices.

These regional offices of the SEC are in New York City, Boston, Atlanta, Chicago, Fort Worth, Denver, Los Angeles and Washington. Information from these reports can be copied for you by the SEC Public Reference Branch, 450 Fifth St., N.W., Washington, DC 20549. In some cases you can get the documents directly from the company involved.

As there are many reference books documenting top business professionals, so there are also directories for many other professional groups. Many will be useful to development officers.

Two major directories list members of the legal profession: *Martindale-Hubbell Law Directory* lists lawyers by law firms geographically. *Who's Who in American Law* follows the usual who's who format with straight alphabetical listing of almost 20,000 lawyers. Both give biographical information, including education and past career positions.

Publications relating to physicians are the *Directory of Medical Specialists* and the membership directory of the American Medical Association. For both the legal and the medical professions there are probably local directories which cover your city or state.

Examples of other major professional directories which give biographical information are *American Men and Women of Science, Directory of American Scholars, American Architects, Contemporary Authors, Who's Who in American Politics, Who's Who in Labor,* and *Who's Who in Real Estate.* Ask a librarian if there is one for a particular profession in which you are interested. Matching the logical profession with your cause may give you a list of persons with a special interest in your subject.

A good reference tool to consult for this is the *Directory of Directories.* Its subtitle calls it "An annotated guide to business and industrial directories, professional and scientific rosters, directory databases, and other lists and guides of all kinds." That is not an unfounded boast. About 8,500 directories are listed with information about each. If you can't find a group which relates to your field, you just aren't trying! There are lists of acaralogists (Okay, maybe you don't need a list of people who study mites and ticks, but isn't it nice to know there is one?) and lists of traveling circuses. Browse through the book at your local library. You won't be disappointed.

Besides these professional directories, there are others which relate to persons involved in philanthropical foundations and organizations. These identify persons with a known interest in giving. *The Foundation Directory* is probably familiar to all fund raisers. It lists information on over 4,000 corporate, community and independent foundations. In addition to this general information on the grant-making history of foundations, there is also a name index which lists donors and foundation officers. *People in Philanthropy*, published by the Washington based Taft Group, lists about 8,000 wealthy people, major donors, private and corporate foundation trustees and administrators of corporate direct-giving programs. It gives name, birthdate and birthplace, education, business and non-profit affiliation, and philanthropic activity. There are separate sections for each category of entry, and indexes which bring together pertinent information. The 1984 volume is expensive, $187, but it may be useful for your office. Earlier editions were called *Trustees of Wealth*.

Another Taft Group publication is *America's Wealthiest People: Their Philanthropic and Nonprofit Affiliations*. It profiles about 500 persons with basic biographical facts and information about their philanthropy. It is designed so fund raisers can look for a "hook" to their own organizations. Indexes are by philanthropic affiliation, by category of non-profit affiliation and by geographical location. It gives an estimate of net worth and makes some comments on the biographee, such as "thought to be civic minded." With this, and other biographical reference works which come out irregularly, watch for outdated information. Look for another source for important details about a person's current status.

A new publication also useful in fund raising is *Foundations,* published in 1984. It is not a guide to current foundation giving such as *The Foundation Directory*. Instead, this book details the history and philosophy of 230 foundations, 227 of which have assets over $30 million. The background information on a foundation's donor, the donor's reasons for forming a foundation, and the history of the foundation's giving patterns all may provide insight for the fund raiser. Even though your request may be for an individual, rather than a foundation contribution, it is useful to know the history of a family's or individual's philanthropy.

Aside from directories which categorize persons by profession or by interest, there are others which list prominent members of particular racial or religious groups.

Although the book is now over 10 years old, a useful directory of prominent Blacks is *Ebony Success Library*. Volume One is *1000 Successful Blacks;* Volume Two is titled *Famous Blacks Give Secrets of Success*. This second volume gives more detailed information on a few persons from volume one. If you wish to contact one of the Black men or women listed in this set, you should use another source to update your information and to find a current address. Many will be in the Marquis publications, or you can use *Who's Who Among Black Americans* which is published every few years. The latter book gives information in a typical who's who format.

A brand-new entry to the listing of successful Black s is *Who's Who of Black Millionaires*. The book has been reviewed as a "vanity salute" to 93 Blacks—36 entertainers, 35 professional and business persons, and 22 athletes. Aside from the typical biographical information, annual income and humanitarian activities are given. Although probably all are listed in other reference books, it may be useful to have this directory of 93 rich Blacks listed together. Except for those directories which are exclusively for one race, none of the standard biographical works list race among the data items.

The May issue of *Ebony* each year lists their choice for the 100 most influential Black Americans. These are listed with name, profession and a brief career notice. Although an address is not included, it is often easy to contact the person through information given, or by consulting other who's who type directories. *Black Enterprise* - "Leading Black Businesses Issue" is the June issue of this periodical. It lists top Black-owned or Black-controlled businesses, banks, savings and loan associations, and insurance companies. The chief executive officer is given.

Another example of a directory which lists individuals from a particular ethnic group is *Who's Who of Sino-Americans*. It is published in both English and Chinese and covers 2,000 Chinese Americans prominent in all fields.

*Who's Who in American Jewry* comes out very irregularly with the latest edition in 1980. It lists 6,000 American Jews. *Who's Who in World Jewry* has not been published recently. It included about 10,000 sketches of living prominent Jewish leaders in various parts of the world, with most living in the United States or Israel. Inclusion is based on influence, position and achievement.

A more selective publication is *American Jewish Biographies* which sketches fewer persons but gives more information on each one. Often, community or philanthropic interests of the person are listed. Many are well-known individuals, but some are lesser-known. About 500 Jews are included.

Directories often exist for members of ethnic organizations for certain professions. An example is *Decalogue Society of Lawyers - Directory of Members*. This is a society of 1,600 lawyers of the Jewish faith. The membership list cannot be purchased, but is available only to members.

*Directorio Profesional Hispano* (Spanish-speaking professionals in Eastern U.S.) covers 3,500 Hispanic doctors, optometrists, dentists, lawyers, architects and accountants with offices in the East. No biographical information is given, just the name, address and phone number, by profession.

If it would be to your advantage for your fund-raising efforts to have information on ethnic groups, you should check *Ethnic Information Sources of the United States*. This covers non-print and print sources of information about ethnic groups representing more than 90 countries, regions or language groups. It includes associations and fraternal organizations as well as a wide variety of other information. By finding if there is an association for a particular ethnic group you could determine if mailing lists or membership directories are available. Blacks, American Indians and Eskimos are omitted because they are well-covered elsewhere. This is published irregularly, with the latest edition in 1983.

Many religious denominations have their own directories or yearbooks which include some biographical information on their leaders. Ask at the religion section of a library to see what church directories are available. Often these books give the church leaders, but these probably are not the most wealthy members of a denomination. If you are even remotely connected to a religious organization, you probably have access to your own church publications. You may not, however, have thought of them as sources of names for your donor list or for information about persons for your board.

College catalogs, which are available in many libraries in print form or on microfilm, list members of the board of trustees of the institution, but few give more biographical information. Some college and university alumni directories are of use to fund raisers. Development officers for a children's hospital use these directories to look up the alma maters and fraternities for members of the hospital board. Those board members then send letters to their old college buddies asking for contributions. The personal touch works, according to those who use it.

You can use those directories for names to contact. You will then have to go elsewhere for more information on the person. Most libraries do not keep college alumni directories, but ask around your organization and you can come up with a few. Check to see if there are local alumni chapters of major universities in your city and then talk to them about their membership lists.

As mentioned earlier, use of national and city social directories can be helpful in identifying wealthy members of your community. They can also be used for seeking more biographical information, although they don't tell very much about a person. Many directories do a pretty good job of listing family residences aside from the main residence and of listing children of the person listed. Some state where the children go to school. Social clubs are usually given. Don't be surprised if the name you seek is not listed in the social directory. Sometimes the social directory publisher has the final say about a person's inclusion, and a nasty divorce or business scandal can erase a name from the listing. If such has recently happened to your searched-for person, look in back editions for information.

Many others are being dropped for any number of reasons, or even non-reasons, according to the *Wall Street Journal*. A November 14, 1984 article reported the 1985 edition will have 3,500 less people than the previous edition. The *Social Register*, which has listed socially prominent people for nearly 100 years, wants to limit its total to 33,000. Part of this reduction may stem from the current emphasis on fame, money, achievement or beauty more than blood lines. Many in the directory use it as a "convenient telephone book" when planning their dinner parties. "Other outsiders," according to the article, "also find it useful—real estate brokers and fund raisers, for example."

Of the 12 with more than $1 billion listed in the *Forbes* list of 400, only one, Gordon Peter Getty, is in the *Social Register*.

In Texas, the state where money seems to talk the loudest, there is the before-mentioned September 1979 issue of *Town and Country* which lists Texans with over $30 million. In Houston a company named WHO Publishing Company has published *WHO Houston* which lists 5,000 residents of Houston whom the publishers have chosen for their social and financial position.

Another company, the old-reliable Debrett's Peerage people in England, has now surfaced in this country. Their hope is that Americans will take money as seriously as the British have taken aristocracy. Debretts will publish a 10-volume series, the Texas volume titled *Debrett's Texas Peerage* concentrates on the "glittering star system of America's social leadership." For Texas, these are mostly the landed and the oiled gentry, with more than 100 Texas families in the category of having $30 million or more.

Watch for upcoming volumes for this set. Both *Debrett's Old South Peerage* and its *California Peerage* are due in 1985. *New*

*York* is scheduled next, with *Boston and New England* following. The series should be completed in 1990. It is doubtful if Americans will ever buy completely the concept of aristocracy as determined by money, but it will be interesting to see these books as a new series on some rich Americans in several geographical areas.

An attempt to document "The 100 Most Generous Living Americans" appeared in the December 1983 issue of *Town and Country*. Starting with Walter Annenberg, who has given away over $100 million, down to those who have given a mere $5 million, the list includes individuals or families who have been the most generous. Research on these top 100 was done in foundation reports, books, news clippings and fund-raising newsletters, said author Dan Rottenberg. He said that what he found may be just the tip of the iceberg. Others who fit into that category may not be listed because of the stiffness of standards for inclusion on this list. Many large gifts are made by anonymous donors also.

Although none of the living Americans equal the $531 million gifts of John D. Rockefeller during his lifetime, there are families which now collectively give more. The Mellon family, according to Rottenberg, has given more than $800 million to worthy causes since World War II.

The *Town and Country* list is fascinating, partly because it includes many names which are not very well-known. It suggests there is lots of money around, waiting to be given to a charity of one's choice! Much of the giving was done regionally—to universities, to art museums and to hospitals—in the person's home town.

The entries for each person on that list tell which organizations or institutions have benefited from the person's generosity. They also tell where the original fortune was made. As such, the article is interesting, almost inspiring, reading for anyone doing development work. Just to see these major gifts documented in one place is a bit awesome. It shows that philanthropy is very much part of the life style of America's rich.

If you missed that *Town and Country* article, look for it in a library. If it is not available there, the individual issue can be ordered by sending a check for $3.75 to Back Issue Department,

Hearst Publications, 250 W. 55th Street, New York, New York, 10019. A call to that department at (212) 262-8485 will determine if the issue is still available. Reprints of individual articles from *Town and Country* are available only for 100 or more copies. A reprint of that article might be an interesting "handout" at a fund-raising convention.

Jacqueline Thompson has written two books on the rich of America. The first, *The Rich and the Super Rich*, is a somewhat gossipy look at lifestyles of those who either inherited or made a lot of money. The newer book is *Future Rich*, a projection of who will have the money around the turn of the century. Included are many names—most of them now not known. They represent new, often high-tech companies. The future rich, Thompson writes, will be the big spenders and the big givers, we can hope, in the future.

*Corporate 500: The Directory of Corporate Philanthropy* is a useful reference source which should be known to most fund raisers. Because the corporate philosophy of philanthropy must originate with, or be carried on by, the current top executives, it is beneficial to know which companies regard philanthropy as an important part of their business. This directory gives the contact person within the corporation who deals with philanthropy. Contribution committee members are listed also.

As there is this listing of corporate giving, there is also *Pacs Americana: A Directory of Political Action Committees and Their Interests*. This spells out those committees which are registered with the Federal Election Commission and gives their sponsoring organizations. It includes a ranked list of the top 100 PAC contributors to federal campaigns.

# 9
# How to Find Donor Family Information

*Wealth is a very dangerous inheritance,*
*unless the inheritor is trained*
*to active benevolence.*

*Charles Simmons*

It is still true that a great many of the persons who have money today got it through heredity. It is very useful, therefore, to be able to find biographical information about the person's family, or about the person who originally made the family fortune. There are many historical reference books which may make it easier to find information on the deceased than on the living. After all, most persons, even the most reclusive, have their lives finally revealed in their obituaries and the information from those obits then gets into historical reference books. These obits most often give family details about relationships which will be useful for the fund raiser. Is the current James Doe related to the well-known John Doe? Is he a brother or a son? What relation is Mary Doe Smith to James Doe? An obit should tell.

The best place to begin is at a library which has the one volume *Historical Biographies Master Index*. Because this indexes the very important *Dictionary of American Biography* (known as the *DAB*), the *National Cyclopedia of American Biography (NCAB)* and *Who Was Who in America (WWWA)*, you will find many names of the deceased persons for whom you are searching. If you don't find the exact individual, you may be able to get your questions answered by reading the entries for other members with the same family name. Besides those major works on deceased persons, the book also indexes several sources which cover significant persons in a particular field.

*Who Was Who in America* is the most extensive listing for deceased Americans. It includes an historical volume which covers persons who died between 1607 and 1896. Since then, seven volumes have been published, listing deaths through 1981. An index to the whole set was published in 1981, making research in that set much easier.

All of these books, the historical volume and the continuing volumes, contain basically the same information as a typical who's who type entry for a living person in *Who's Who in America*. As the historical volume predates the *WWA* volumes, the information for that volume was gathered from other sources. The later volumes usually just add a death date to the last entry in the *WWA* which appeared during the person's life. A person is entered on confirmation of death, or when a person is assumed to be dead because the birth date was over 100 years ago. Some living persons, however, end up as "has beens" in *WWWA*. One man appeared at my reference desk and showed me his entry in *WWWA*. He wasn't 100-years-old, nor was he dead. If there is a death date, you can be sure the person is dead. If no death date appears, be a bit cautious and look around for more information before you refer to the late Mr. So and So.

Another quirk of this set, which is normally very reliable, is that the *WWWA* entry is often not updated at the time of the person's death. The original entry may be from many, many years before death, and thus it doesn't include information for those later years. One woman called the library and was pleased to hear that her late author husband was listed in a recent volume of *WWWA*. When she came in to photocopy the entry, she was less than delighted to find that she was not listed as her husband's wife. Only his first wife was listed. Neither she nor her and her husband's children were included. The entry was from the 1930s when her husband, still married to wife number one, had won a literary award. After that moment of limited fame, he was dropped from subsequent volumes of *WWA,* but that entry was used in *WWWA.*

Look at each entry with some caution. If nothing about the person is listed for the last 30 years, look elsewhere for more information.

For persons who have been the most noteworthy in their field, the most prestigious and scholarly American biographical dictionary is the *Dictionary of American Biography.* This most important of historical reference works listing Americans includes those who have been dead several years. This enables the editors to accurately determine that person's place in history. There is an original set, with supplements every few years. The latest, supplement seven, covers persons who died up to 1965. An index to the complete set was published in 1981. A bibliography follows each entry.

Because only the most noteworthy get into *DAB,* you are more apt to find the names you seek in the *National Cyclopedia of American Biography.* 63 volumes of the main set have been published, with 13 volumes in a "current" series which includes living persons. This includes many more names than the *DAB* because it is less selective. Most entries are written from information submitted by family members, so it often mentions the generous deeds of the deceased. For the same reason, the entries often give good family information about children and ancestry. Like the *DAB,* it is written in narrative form, and it outlines the career of the deceased person. Often there is a photograph of the person.

Because each volume of the set is not in alphabetical or any other order, it is necessary to use the very complete *National*

*Cyclopedia of American Biography Index,* published in 1984. This index picks up names other than just those of the main entry, and includes names of businesses and other institutions with which the deceased was involved.

As *NCAB* is a very expensive set, it may not be available in most public libraries. It will, however, be somewhere in each state and will be available through a regional or state library system. Photocopies of the entries needed can be obtained for a small fee. Use the readily available *Historical Biographies Master Index* to find the names you need in this set if you do not have access to the *NCAB*'s own index.

Women and minorities are often sadly missing, in the numbers which represent their importance, from both of the previously mentioned historical sets. There are now separate sets to somewhat correct this omission.

*Notable American Women, 1607-1950, A Biographical Dictionary* covers women who died before the end of 1950. *Notable American Women: The Modern Period* covers those who died between 1951 and 1975. A fund raiser might use these works to find biographical and historical family information on an ancestor of the person now being researched.

In some cases, the person documented in this set is actually the one who made the fortune; in some cases she is a relative of those who did. To note the difference, you can use the very good classified vocational index at the end of Volume Three of the main set, and at the end of the volume for the modern period. In those indexes there is a heading called "Philanthropists." The entries for those so listed are fascinating, and will surely interest anyone active in current development work. There are 59 women in the philanthropist listing in the main set; 16 in the modern period. In that later volume, there are entries for such women as the cosmetics tycoon Helena Rubinstein; the fantastically generous Texan, Ima Hogg; and the music patron, Mary Louise Curtis Bok Zimbalist. Each of these 75 women have entries which give patterns of their giving as well as their rationale for their philanthropy. This information is often hard to find in other books, so these articles can be read for their philanthropic philosophy as well as for their biographical information. You can hope the living descendent of those earlier generous women will carry on the family traditions.

Each article on those notable women includes a bibliography. Each is well-researched and well-written by those who have evaluated an entry as well as given biographical information on the women.

What that set does for women, the *Dictionary of American Negro Biography* does for Blacks who died before 1970. This volume includes not only all of the well-known important Blacks, but also many generally unheard of until their lives were documented in this work. Some of those included here accumulated a great deal of wealth in their times and many were generous with it. The volume was originally published without a classified index, but one is now available in later printings.

Those sets represent only the most distinguished deceased Americans. Many others may have had considerable wealth but they are not in these books. Many of them may have had obituaries in the *New York Times,* and thus can be easily researched through the *New York Times Obituaries Index, 1858-1968* or in the second volume which covers 1969-1978. The basic volume lists over 353,000 names listed under "Deaths" in the newspaper. Sometimes, even if you do not have access to the complete file of that newspaper on microfilm it will be helpful to know the exact date of death. You can then find an obit for that person, by using the date, in a less-well-indexed newspaper.

One quirk of this index is that if a person is prominent enough to have information on his or her death on the front page of the *New York Times,* or on a page other than with the obits, it may not be picked up in this index. In cases of a person that prominent, however, you will probably have no trouble finding the necessary death date elsewhere.

Sometimes the obituary information is exactly what a fund raiser would have liked to know about the person when he or she was still able to write checks. They also may give a philosophy of philanthrophy which may be carried on to living members of the family being researched.

An example of this type of obit was one of the most interesting I have seen about a philanthropist. It was a 1965 obit for a Dr. Leonard Fuld, hardly a name known to every fund raiser. Dr. Fuld gave away about a million dollars each year during the last 35 years of his life. Most of the money was given to schools of nursing along the East Coast. His method of approach was rather unusual. He would appear in the hospital's reception room and ask about the health of the student nurses. Because of his shabby appearance and strange question, he was often ejected from the property. If he wasn't thrown out, he often gave that hospital a new nurses' dormitory, a scholarship program, or even a new hospital wing. More than 20 hospitals benefited from the generosity of this elderly man who never explained why he was so interested in the welfare of nurses. He denied ever having been in love with one, a question he was often asked.

As interesting as his case is, it would have been very difficult, probably impossible, for any fund raiser to find information on him during his lifetime. He was a publicity-shy bachelor who forever surprised people with his vast knowledge on a variety of subjects. He had several degrees from Columbia, including a Ph.D., but people who had dealings with him for many years never knew it. Most of his life he lived in a tenement building in Harlem, performing janitorial services in the building he owned. After his death it was revealed that he had made a fortune in real estate and the stock market. In fact, one of his unusual gifts was to give to the Wharton School of Finance and Commerce, as it was known then, one share from each company sold on the New York Stock Exchange in 1958. Not only did this bring in some dividend income, but it also provided an opportunity for business students to study the annual reports from each company.

If you have a mysterious donor among your contributors, someone about whom you can find nothing, the best advice is not to worry about it. Enjoy the person's gifts, but don't try to figure it out. Perhaps when the person dies, the obituary will tell you all you want to know. The person may even be as generous in death, through his will, as he was in life. You can only hope so. By saying this, I'm aware that I'm contradicting John D. Rockefeller, Jr.'s theory that the more you know about a donor, the better your success with him will be.

Because of the good index, the obituaries from the *New York Times* are the most useful, but there are other records of obituaries which may be helpful. *Obituaries on File*, a two-volume set which covers deaths between 1940 to 1978, gives a very brief sketch about the person, and lists the date and place of death. It includes about 25,000 names, and may serve as a first-step in finding more information about a person listed here.

There are also books which give dates of death for persons in specific fields. One is *Who Was Who on Screen*. Another is *Variety Obits*, which gives the date an obituary of a performer appeared in *Variety* magazine.

*Notable Names In American History* serves a very useful function if you think the ancestor you are researching may have held a high government position, been the president of a university, a governor or mayor, or held any high position. This book lists who held what position, in chronological order, from the time the position was established until the 1970s. Answers to questions such as "Was the man I'm looking for really the Secretary of the Treasury under President Hoover?" are quickly answered by this volume. After you get that fact right, your research can proceed elsewhere for more information.

Another good source for deceased Americans is *Appleton's Cyclopaedia of American Biography* which sometimes includes names not found in the other historical volumes. This is also indexed in *Historical Biographies Master Index* and, although it is old, it is a classic reference set found in many libraries.

There are also many reference sources which list prominent deceased persons in a particular field. Perhaps the most useful set for fund raisers will be the *Biographical Dictionary of American Business Leaders*. This four-volume set is the most comprehensive coverage of business leaders, from colonial times to the present. Although most of those included are deceased, there are a few leaders who are still alive. This set has a good index including listings of women, Blacks and other business leaders by geographical locations. If several members of one family were involved in the same business, there are family listings instead of just individual listings. This is useful in sorting out those sometimes confusing relationship questions. Those you are researching may be the descendants of the business leaders in this set. This may explain the origins of the family wealth.

Other fields are also well covered with retrospective biographical reference works. There is a *World Who's Who in Science* and a much more exclusive *Dictionary of Scientific Biography,* which covers the field back to ancient times but includes only the most important names.

For American politicians of the past there is the *Biographical Directory of the American Congress* as well as the *Biographical Directory of the Governors of the United States, 1790-1978* and the *Biographical Dictionary of American Mayors, 1820-1980.*

There are historical volumes of educators, economists, librarians, musicians, actors and actresses, movie stars, composers, psychologists, athletes, labor leaders, comedians and almost every other profession. If you are looking for information on someone who isn't in the general biographical guides, check to see if there might be a special directory for persons in a particular field.

Try these directories of deceased persons if the individual you are researching is from "old money" or is a member of a distinguished family. You will discover that information on former generations will help deal with the current donor.

For searching family information which will link the original fortune-maker to the present generations, it is useful to use all of the other methods discussed in previous chapters. Many current foundations were formed by persons now deceased, but the philosophy of the foundation continues, in most cases, to be that of the original funder. Look through biographical directories published during the lifetime of the foundation donor. Also check for periodical articles and newspaper clippings. Check the person's obituary. When the deceased person is well-documented, then focus your attention on current members of that family. Many of them will still be in the news, if not listed in biographical directories.

A recent question we had at the library concerned information on contributors to a foundation established about 20 years ago by a couple who were killed in an airplane crash. What could we find about the couple, known to be very publicity shy, and whatever happened to the couple's children? Reports of the plane crash and the couple's obituary told most of the story. An article on one daughter told the history of what had happened to the family since the plane crash. Usually a combination of research methods is necessary. No one source is sufficient to answer a multi-faceted question.

The more you do this type of research the better you will become at it. You will pick up clues along the way which will help you and the librarian go on to the next clue. Even if you meet an occasional "dead end," you will probably have gathered some useful information along the way which will be of help in doing the next biographical search for your organization.

# 10
# How to Search For Information by Computer

*Higher productivity levels aren't achieved by working harder, but rather by using more efficient means to meet goals and a better organization of time.*

*Dennis Sullivan*

No directory which identifies reference tools used for biographical or any other kind of research can be complete without information about the relatively new field of online research. The possibilities are overwhelming! What used to take hours is now done in minutes, and done much more thoroughly. Informational materials in research centers throughout the country are now available elsewhere through the new technologies of online computer searching. Information in regional newspapers is now immediately available elsewhere in the country through many online services which index, abstract, or provide the full text of news articles. Access can be by any combination of key words or, for biographical research, by person's name.

Keep in mind that information retrieval through online searching is changing constantly. What is not available one month may be available the next. For biographical searching the best advice is to ask for help at the library where you normally get your information. It doesn't matter much what type of library that is, although some are much more sophisticated than others in this new technology. Often that depends on how "rich" the library is. Online research can be expensive. Some libraries use the new technologies, then rely on other libraries for the basic reference books which are indexed by computer services. Many government libraries have access to databases but no longer purchase the books which they index. Messengers are sent to the public library to photocopy what is needed by government agencies.

Libraries, even some rather small public libraries with limited funding, are becoming more and more dependent on online databases for which they pay a designated connect-time fee. Sometimes that fee is paid by the user; sometimes the library absorbs the fee. Most larger public libraries are now wrestling with the right approach, as are other research libraries. Clients are discovering it is actually cheaper to pay the fee for prompt service, and libraries are able to increase their efficiency by offering online facilities. Fees can range from $15 to $100 per hour for connect time, $60 per hour is average. That may sound quite steep, but a skilled librarian can identify the necessary information in seconds or, at least, in a few minutes.

Each fund raiser must decide if the cost is justified. How much value can be attached to a piece of research? If the information found through online searching leads to a sizable contribution, the research was definitely worth the investment. Even if it does not, the cost can be justified in terms of staff time. In most cases the research will be much more thorough than that done manually. A study done in 1983 estimated that a brief 40-minute trip to a library cost a total of $10.27 in terms of travel cost and the hourly wage of the person who made the trip. Obtaining the equivalent information from a database could have cost only $2.61. What sometimes can take staff half a day at a large downtown library can be done in minutes on a computer.

If your development office is connected with an institution which has online capabilities, by all means use them for your development and fund-raising research. Engage the person or persons who normally uses the equipment by explaining what information you need, then let him or her put the computer through its paces. You will be astonished by the results!

More and more old-line publishing companies are now online. As mentioned, *Who's Who in America* is a good reference book to use to begin your research. The online version is also a good place to begin. The Marquis Who's Who Database is available through DIALOG, an information retrieval service which is used extensively throughout the country by all types of libraries and corporate offices. This offers the capability of putting together lists of possible donors according to many keywords, and saves hours and hours of staff time doing a job which is almost impossible without a computer. This database began with the 1982 edition of *Who's Who in America* and later added the new *Who's Who in Frontier Science and Technology*. As new editions are published, the database is updated, and other publications will be added later. The researcher using the service through DIALOG can, for a fee, put together lists of persons in any number of categories to meet individual organization's needs.

Information is grouped into several categories of information: vital statistics, such as name, birth city, birth state and year of birth; career information, such as company name, company location, occupation name, and position held; education information; achievements, such as awards, honors, etc.; professional memberships and religious affiliations; family information; and address information.

Imagine the possibilities for fund-raising research. You could get a list of company executives in a particular area who have included a particular activity, such as an arts organization, in their civic activities. You could get degree holders from a particular educational institution, female chief executive officers under the age of 40, *WWA* listees who live in Baltimore, Jewish persons in Connecticut, or Lutherans in Minnesota.

If you want just biographical information on a particular person who is listed in *WWA*, use the print edition. If you want to put together a listing of names to fit your needs and you have access to a computer, use the *WWA* database. Some of the same information can be obtained through the various print indexes provided by Marquis, but using them does not provide the various combinations which can be gathered by the computer.

Another service provided by Marquis is *Who's Who Information Service,* a custom search by Marquis staff who will put together information from their database for customers. For example, you could ask for a list of graduates from your college or university, or for a listing of prominent persons from your congressional district, or a list of lawyers born in your state.

According to the Marquis catalog, the uses of these *WWA* database services are to "research backgrounds of notables prior to contact" and to "identify potential board members and donors." It states that "alumni and development officers, executive recruiters, foundations and fund raisers can benefit from this new service."

If it sounds useful for your purposes, call for more information and get an estimate of costs. Call 1-800-621-9669 or write to Marquis Who's Who Inc., 200 East Ohio Street, Chicago, IL 60611.

Also available through DIALOG is the very useful *Biography Master Index* provided from Gale Research Company. This puts almost two million names into one index and tells where to find further information on the person. *American Men and Women in Science* is available online. Both *Foundation Directory* and *Foundations Grants Index* will give information on philanthropic foundations through DIALOG.

Each year more and more files are being added to informational retrieval services such as DIALOG. For more information, call 415-858-3785 or write to DIALOG Information Services, Inc., 3460 Hillview Avenue, Palo Alto, CA 94304.

As one would imagine, the whole area of business information access is very well covered by online search databases. One database, available through DIALOG, is "Disclosure II" which includes such things as proxy statements and other U.S. Securities and Exchange Commission required reports. Ask around to see what business services may be available in your area. Sometimes the business community helps the public library pay for these databases and they may be available there, either for free use or for a fee. Either way, it may be the cheapest way to get the answers quickly.

Standard and Poor's Corporation also offers a computer-based information service called Compmark Data Services. This identifies and makes available information, for a service fee, on 400,000 top corporate executives from 40,000 companies. As with other computer services, information can be accessed several ways. Among those are professional rank, home address, college or university attended, or memberships on boards. The information received is basically what is available in the *Standard and Poor's Register,* but the advantage in this system is that it can bring together lists of executives in various fields much faster and much more accurately than one would be able to do without the computer. Call the Standard and Poor's Corporation at 212-248-2525.

The Securities and Exchange Commission has awarded a contract to Computer Directions Advisors to compile and make commercially available information from forms which are required by the SEC. Many of these forms contain information on the net worth of individuals. The *Spectrum* series is available online and in publication form. It reports the holdings and changes in holdings of common stocks and convertibles as reported by the SEC. Most useful, for your purposes, are *Spectrum* 5 and *Spectrum* 6.

*Spectrum* 5 alphabetically lists by common stock all owners of 5% or more of the outstanding shares of any U.S. publicly held corporation.

*Spectrum* 6 gives information on company insiders. Officers, directors and 10% principal stockholders of companies registered with the SEC are listed alphabetically by common stock, with number of shares held.

These reports can be sorted geographically to show owners in specific metropolitan areas and alphabetically by name for five percent owners and company insiders.

For more information on this service, how it can be accessed and how it could benefit your organization, contact Computer Directions Advisors, Inc., 11501 Georgia Avenue, Silver Spring, MD 20902. The telephone is (301) 942-1700.

If what you need is a search for newspaper articles which tell about your subject, then there are fantastic possibilities online.

As newspapers entered the electronic age in the 1960s, many converted to photo-electric equipment to set type and print papers. This made it possible to collect articles into an electronic library. Originally these libraries were used only by their own newspaper staff. Soon it became apparent that this gathered information had a marketing potential and it was made accessible through computerization. In 1969 the *New York Times* was the first to market this information. Since then many other newspapers are now available online. What was available originally was just an abstracting of articles. Now, in many cases, the whole article is available and key words are very well indexed to access the articles.

The *New York Times Online Data Base* was begun in 1980 with the full-text version of the *Times*. In 1983 this was added to a service provided by Mead Data, a communications company which was marketing full-text articles from major newspapers throughout the country. This service, through its information services NEXIS, offers extraordinary online information, up to the minute. If the name you search has been in one of the covered newspapers, the computer search will find it. In January 1984 NEXIS contained 15 large city newspapers, and is now available through DIALOG and other information service companies.

Okay, that covers the big newspapers, but what if the names you need are from newspapers in Oklahoma or Nebraska or Maryland? In 1982, Knight-Ridder met that need also. It marketed a service called *VU-Text* which picked up dozens of other newspapers which had electronic newsrooms.

Aside from these services which offer full text for the articles, there are also possibilities for online index searching. *Magazine*

*Index, Business Index* and *National Newspaper Index* are available through DIALOG and other companies. *Newspaper Index (NDEX)* is a service which indexes citations to 10 major U.S. newspapers serving Black Americans. *Wilsonline* is a new service which puts into a database the old-reliable H.W.Wilson Company periodical indexes which have been used in libraries around the country since 1898.

If you have no access to online computers, nor any libraries in your area which offer these possibilities, you can still investigate using computers for your research through an information broker. Your telephone directory may list those in your area under that term or under terms such as research services or research companies. Another way to find a list is by using the *National Directory of Addresses and Telephone Numbers.* Check under database information services and research services. (Aside from this use, you may wish to check that directory for a host of other useful information.)

Computers are drastically changing methods for gathering and storing information. Perhaps, with your office computer, you may wish to store the information in a database, rather than on personal data sheets in your files. Many companies provide assistance in setting up office procedures which make the files available under specific categories for your fund raising or development uses.

# Epilogue

A few years ago at the public library we received calls for a book titled "Who's Who in Philanthropy." I had never heard of it, but the callers were always sure that it existed. I did some investigation, but never found a publication even slightly resembling this magical book which would list those who had the money and wanted to give it away. I suspect the callers were fund raisers reacting to a rumor about the existence of such a book, or perhaps they were responding to a strong case of wishful thinking. Maybe someone, somewhere, really did publish such a book, but it did not get wide distribution. It probably wasn't very good. Such a book would be too good to be true, and fund raising is never that simple.

No such book, at least not a really comprehensive book, could be written unless every organization and institution were willing to share their good friends and big donors with others. Most aren't that benevolent. Nor would one's large donors necessarily be of any help to others. Many donors give most generously to their own pet causes or to organizations with whom they have been previously involved.

News of big gifts given to organizations and institutions does get around. Such news probably does bring forth a surge of requests for help from others. Until the list of big donors was published in the December 1983 issue of *Town and Country*, it was harder to identify the super-donors even though the American Association of Fund-Raising Counsel in New York keeps tab on national fund-raising totals. Large donations are also listed in the monthly *Philanthropic Digest*.

Without a "Who's Who in Philanthropy," development officers and fund raisers will have to use their ingenuity to discover names of prospective donors and board members. After they have the name, they will have to continue to use some skill in finding biographical information on that person to connect him or her to the organization's mission. These professional fund seekers must be a little like a plucky bird which inhabits shorelines along both North American coasts. This little bird, the ruddy turnstone, seeks its food by turning over and looking under stones and pebbles on the beach. Fund raisers must also leave no stone unturned in their search for biographical information on donors to their organization's cause.

# Bibliography

*Access: The Supplementary Index to Periodicals.* Gaylord, Syracuse, NY. 1975-date.

*American Architects Directory.* Bowker, New York. 1956-date.

American Medical Association. *American Medical Directory.* American Medical Association, Chicago. 1906-date.

*American Men and Women of Science.* Bowker, New York. 1971-date. (Was *American Men of Science.* 1906-1968).

*America's Wealthiest People: Their Philanthropic and Nonprofit Affiliations.* Taft Group, 5125 MacArthur Blvd., Washington, DC 20016. 1984.

*Angels (Theater and Film Backers).* Leo Shull Publications, 1501 Broadway, New York, NY 10036. Annual, September.

*Annual Register of Grant Support: A Directory of Funding Sources.* Marquis, Chicago. 1969-date.

*Appleton's Cyclopaedia of American Biography,* ed. by J.G. Wilson and John Fiske. Appleton, New York. 1894-1900.

*Ayer Directory of Publications.* Ayer, Philadelphia. 1880-date.

Best, Hugh. *Debrett's Texas Peerage.* Coward-McCann, New York. 1984.

*Biographical Dictionary of American Mayors, 1820-1981.* Greenwood, Westport, CT. 1980.

*Biographical Directory of the American Congress, 1774-1971.* GPO, Washington. 1971.

*Biographical Directory of the Governors of the United States, 1789-1978.* Meckler

Books, Westport, CT. 1978.

*Biography Almanac.* Gale, Detroit. 1983.

*Biography and Genealogy Master Index: A Consolidated Index to More Than 3,200,000 Biographical Sketches in Over 350 Current and Retrospective Biographical Dictionaries,* 2nd ed. Gale, Detroit. 1980.

*Biography Index: A Cumulative Index to Biographical Material in Books and Magazines.* H.W. Wilson, New York. 1947-date.

*Black Enterprise*—"Leading Black Businesses Issue." Earl G. Graves Publishing Company, 295 Madison Avenue, New York, NY 10017. Annual, June.

Brownstone, David and Carruth, Gorton. *Where to Find Business Information: A Worldwide Guide for Everyone Who Needs the Answers to Business Questions.* Wiley, New York. 1982.

*Business Index.* Information Access Company, 11 Davis Drive, Belmont, CA 94002. 1980-date.

*Business Periodicals Index.* H.W. Wilson, New York. 1958-date.

*Business Week*—"Annual Survey of Executive Compensation Issue." McGraw-Hill, New York. Annual, a May issue.

Chandler, David. *Dialing for Data: A Consumer's How-To Handbook on Computer Communications.* Random House, New York. 1984.

*Christian Science Monitor Index,* 1950-date. Bell & Howell, Wooster, OH. 1961-date.

*Congressional District Zip Codes.* Tyson Capitol Institute, 7735 Old Georgetown Road, Bethesda, MD 20814. Biennial.

*Contacts Influential.* Contacts Influential International Corporation, 20950 Center Ridge Road, Suite 106, Cleveland, OH 44116. Irregular.

*Contemporary Authors.* Gale, Detroit. 1962-date.

*Cordovan Business Journals.* Cordovan Business Journals, 5314 Bingle Road, P.O. 10973, Houston, TX 77292. Separate journals for 12 areas. Weekly.

*Corporate 500: The Directory of Corporate Philanthropy.* Public Management Institute, 358 Brannan Street, San Francisco, CA 94107. 1980-date. Annual.

Cunningham, Amy. "Can You Write A Check for, Say $10,000?", *Washingtonian,* December 1982, pg. 103 + .

*Current Biography.* H.W. Wilson, New York. 1940-date.

*Current Biography Cumulated Index, 1940-1970.* H.W. Wilson, New York. 1971.

Davis, William. *The Rich: A Study of the Species.* Franklin Watt, New York. 1983.

*Decalogue Society of Lawyers—Directory of Members*. Decalogue Society of Lawyers, 180 W. Washington Street, Chicago, IL 60602. 1983.

*Dictionary of American Biography*. Scribner, New York. 1928-date.

*Dictionary of American Biography. Complete Index Guide to Volumes I-X, Supplements 1-7*. Scribner, New York. 1981.

*Dictionary of Scientific Biography*. Scribner, New York. 1970-1980.

*Direct Mail List Rates and Data*. Standard Rate and Data Service, Inc., 5201 Old Orchard Road, Skokie, IL 60077. Quarterly.

*Directorio Profesional Hispano (Spanish-Speaking Professionals in Eastern U.S.)*. Blanca Balbi, Box 408, Flushing, NY 11352. Annual, October.

*Directory of American Scholars: A Biographical Directory*. Bowker, New York. 1942-date.

*Directory of Directories, 1985. An Annotated Guide to Business and Industrial Directories, Professional and Scientific Rosters, Directory of Databases, and Other Lists and Guides of All Kinds*, 3rd ed. Gale, Detroit. 1984.

*Directory of Medical Specialists*. Marquis, Chicago. 1939-date. Biennial.

*Directory of Women in Marquis Who's Who Publications*. Marquis, Chicago. 1983.

*Dun and Bradstreet Million Dollar Directory*. Dun and Bradstreet, New York. 1985.

*Dun and Bradstreet Reference Book of Corporate Managements*. Dun and Bradstreet, New York. 1967-date. Annual.

*Ebony*—"100 Most Influential Black American Issue". Johnson Publishing Company, 820 S. Michigan Avenue, Chicago, IL 60605. Annual, May.

*Ebony Success Library. v.1. 1,000 Successful Blacks* and *v.2. Famous Blacks Give Secrets of Success*. Southwestern Co., Nashville, TN. 1973.

*Encyclopedia of Associations*. Gale, Detroit. 1956-date. Annual.

*Ethnic Information Sources of the United States*. Gale, Detroit. 1983.

*Forbes*—"Chief Executive Compensation Survey Issue." Forbes, Inc., 60 Fifth Avenue, New York, NY 10011. Annual, a June issue.

*Forbes*—"Forbes Four Hundred Issue (Wealthy Americans)." Forbes, Inc., 60 Fifth Avenue, New York, NY 10011. Annual, a fall issue.

*Foundation Directory*. Foundation Center, New York. 1960-date.

*Haines Criss-Cross Directories*. Haines and Co., 8050 Freedom Avenue N.W., North Canton, OH 44720. Annual.

Harrop, David. *World Pay-Checks: Who Makes What, Where and Why*. Facts on File, New York. 1982.

Hickey, James and Koochoo, Elizabeth. *Prospecting: Searching Out the Philanthropic Dollar*. Taft Group, 5125 MacArthur Blvd., N.W., Washington, DC 20016. 1984.

Horowitz, Lois. *Knowing Where to Look: The Ultimate Guide to Research.* Writer's Digest Books, Cincinnati, OH. 1984.

*How to Reach Anyone Who's Anyone.* Price/Stern/Sloan, Los Angeles, CA. 1980.

Ingham, John N. *Biographical Dictionary of American Business Leaders.* Greenwood, Westport, CT. 1983.

*International Who's Who.* Europa Publications, London. 1935-date.

Johnson, Frank F. *Who's Who of Black Millionaires.* Who's Who of Black Millionaires, P.O. Box 12092, Fresno, CA 93776. 1984.

Keele, Harold and Kiger, Joseph, eds. *Foundations.* Greenwood, Westport, CT. 1984.

Konolige, Kit. *The Richest Women in the World.* Macmillan, New York. 1985.

*Lathrop Report on Newspaper Indexes.* Norman Lathrop Enterprises, P.O. Box 198, Wooster, OH 55691. 1979.

Levine, Michael. *The Address Book: How to Reach Anyone Who's Anyone.* Putnam, New York. 1984.

Logan, Rayford W. and Winston, Michael R., eds. *Dictionary of American Negro Biography.* Norton, New York. 1982.

*Magazine Index.* Information Access Company, 11 Davis Drive, Belmont, CA 94002. 1979-date.

McNeil, Barbara and Herbert, Miranda, eds. *Historical Biographical Dictionaries Master Index.* Gale, Detroit. 1980.

*Marquis Who's Who Publications Index to All Books.* Marquis, Chicago, 1974-date. Biennial.

*Martindale-Hubbell Law Directory.* Martindale-Hubbell, Inc., Box 1001, Summit, NJ 07901. 1931-date. Annual.

Milner, Anita Cheek. *Newspaper Indexes: A Location and Subject Guide for Researchers.* Scarecrow, Metuchen, NJ. 1982.

Moskowitz, Milton, et al. *Everybody's Business: An Almanac. The Irreverent Guide to Corporate America.* Harper and Row, New York. 1983.

*National Cyclopedia of American Biography.* James T. White, Clifton, NJ 07013. 1892-1984.

*National Cyclopedia of American Biography, Index.* James T. White, Clifton, NJ 07013. 1984.

*National Directory of Addresses and Telephone Numbers.* Concord Reference Books, Inc., New York. 1985.

*National Newspaper Index.* Information Access Company, 11 Davis Drive, Belmont, CA 94002. 1979-date. (Microfilm and online index to the

*Christian Science Monitor,* the *New York Times,* the *Los Angeles Times,* the *Wall Street Journal* and the *Washington Post.*)

*New York Times Biographical Edition: A Compilation of Current Biographical Information of General Interest.* Times, New York. 1970-date.

*New York Times Index.* Times, New York. 1913-date. (Prior Series 1851-1912 available on microfilm.)

*New York Times Obituaries Index, 1858-1968.* Times, New York. 1970.

*New York Times Obituaries Index, 1969-1978.* Times, New York, 1980.

*News Bank.* New Canaan, CT. 1983-date.

*Newspaper Index,* Bell & Howell, Wooster, OH. 1972-date. (Indexes the *Chicago Tribune,* the *Los Angeles Times,* the *New Orleans Times-Picayune,* the *Washington Post.*)

*Notable American Women, 1607-1950, A Biographical Dictionary.* Belknap Press of Harvard University Press, Cambridge, MA. 1971.

*Notable American Women, The Modern Period.* Belknap Press of Harvard University Press, Cambridge, MA. 1980.

*Notable Names in American History.* James T. White, Clifton, NJ 07013. 1973.

*Obituaries on File.* Facts on File, New York. 1979.

*Pacs Americana: A Directory of Political Action Committees and their Interests.* Sunshine Services Corporation, 325 Pennsylvania Avenue S.E., Washington, DC 20003. 1984.

Panas, Jerold. *Mega Gifts: Who Gives Them, Who Gets Them.* Pluribus Press, 160 East Illinois St., Chicago, IL 60611. 1984.

Pendleton, Niel. *Fund Raising: A Guide for Non-Profit Organizations.* Prentice Hall, Englewood Cliffs, NJ. 1981.

*People in Philanthropy: A Guide to Philanthropic Leaders, Major Donors, and Funding Connections.* Taft Group, 5125 MacArthur Blvd. N.W., Washington, DC 20016. 1984.

Perry, Jeb H. *Variety Obits: An Index to Obituaries in VARIETY, 1905-1978.* Scarecrow, Metuchen, NJ. 1980.

*Personal Name Index to the New York Times Index.* Roxbury Data Interface, Verdi, NV. 1976-1984.

*Philanthropic Digest.* Brakeley, John Price Jones, Inc., 1100 17th St. N.W., Washington, DC 20036. Monthly.

Polner, Murray. *American Jewish Biographies.* Facts on File, New York. 1982.

*Readers' Guide to Periodical Literature.* H.W. Wilson, New York. 1905-date.

Rose, Louis J. *How to Investigate Your Friends and Enemies.* Albion Press, P.O. Box 445, Exton, PA 19341. 1983.

Rottenberg, Dan. "The Most Generous Living Americans," *Town and Country,* December 1983, pg. 197 +.

*Social Register.* Social Register Association, 381 Park Avenue So., New York, NY 10016. Annual.

*Standard & Poor's Register of Corporations, Directors and Executives, United States and Canada.* Standard & Poor's Corporation, 25 Broadway, New York, NY 10004. Annual.

*Taft Trustees of Wealth: A Biographical Directory of Private Foundation and Corporate Foundation Officers,* 5th ed. Taft Group, 5125 MacArthur Blvd., N.W., Washington, DC 20016. 1979.

Thompson, Jacqueline. *The Very Rich Book: America's Supermillionaires and Their Money — Where They Got It, How They Spend It.* Morrow, New York. 1981.

Thompson, Jacqueline. *Future Rich.* Morrow, New York. 1985.

Truitt, Evelyn Mack. *Who Was Who on Screen,* 3rd ed. Bowker, New York. 1983.

*Wall Street Journal Index,* 1958-date. Dow Jones, New York. 1959-date.

Warner, Irving. *The Art of Fund Raising.* Bantam Books, New York, 1984.

*WHO Houston (Texas).* WHO Publishing Company, 9601 Katy Freeway, Suite 370, Houston, TX 77024. 1984.

*Who Was Who in America: A Companion Biographical Reference Work to Who's Who in America.* Marquis, Chicago. 1942-date.

*Who Was Who in America: Historical Volume, 1607-1896.* Marquis, Chicago. 1963.

*Who Was Who in America With World Notables. Index 1607-1981.* Marquis, Chicago. 1981.

*Who's Who Among Black Americans,* 3rd ed. Educational Communications, 721 N. McKinley, Lake Forest, IL 60045. 1981.

*Who's Who in America.* Marquis, Chicago. 1899-date. Biennial.

*Who's Who in America Birthdate Index.* Marquis, Chicago. 1983.

*Who's Who in America College Alumni Directory.* Marquis, Chicago. 1983.

*Who's Who in America Professional/Geographic Index.* Marquis, Chicago. 1984.

*Who's Who in American Jewry.* Standard Who's Who, 11980 San Vicente Blvd., Suite 111, Los Angeles, CA. 1980.

*Who's Who in American Law.* Marquis, Chicago. 1977-date.

*Who's Who in American Politics: A Biographical Directory of United States Political Leaders.* Bowker, New York. 1967-date. Biennial.

*Who's Who in Finance and Industry.* Marquis, Chicago. 1974-date.

*Who's Who in Labor.* Arno Press, New York. 1976.

*Who's Who in Real Estate.* Warren, Gorham & Lamont, Inc., 210 South Street, Boston, MA 02111. 1983.

*Who's Who in Religion.* Marquis, Chicago. 1975-date.

*Who's Who in the East.* Marquis, Chicago. 1943-date. Biennial.

*Who's Who in the Midwest.* Marquis, Chicago. 1949-date. Biennial.

*Who's Who in the South and Southwest.* Marquis, Chicago. 1950-date. Biennial.

*Who's Who in the West.* Marquis, Chicago. 1949-date. Biennial.

*Who's Who in the World.* Marquis, Chicago. 1970-date.

*Who's Who in Washington.* Tiber Press, 4340 East-West Highway, No. 514, Bethesda, MD 20814. 1983.

*Who's Who in World Jewry.* Pitman, New York. 1972. Discontinued.

*Who's Who of American Women.* Marquis, Chicago. 1958-date.

*Who's Who of Sino-Americans.* Chieng Hua News, P.O. Box 61, Flushing, NY 11352. 1984.

Withey, Henry F. and Withey, Elise. *Biographical Dictionary of American Architects (Deceased).* New Age Publishing Co., Los Angeles. 1956.

*World Who's Who in Science.* Marquis, Chicago. 1968.

Wright, John. *American Almanac of Jobs and Salaries.* Avon Books, New York. 1984.

# Index

.

# Order Form

Please send me _____ copies of

**Where the Money Is**
**A Fund Raiser's Guide to the Rich**
by Helen Bergan
at $12.95 each.

Subtotal _____

Shipping: Please add $1.00 for first copy; 50¢ for each additional copy.

_____

Tax: Virginia residents add 4% state sales tax, 52¢ for each copy.

_____

Total enclosed _____

Name: _____

Address: _____

City/State/Zip _____

Send order to: BioGuide Press
                 P.O. Box 16072-B
                 Alexandria, VA 22302